More Praise for *A New Theology*

Where are words for our deepest sorrow? Where is language that allows us to live without our loved ones? In prose that's heartbreakingly clear, Sheila Bender invites readers along on her journey. She's honest about the stunned confusion, the denial, the futile hope that somehow her fatally injured son might recover. She opens her heart to write the wrenching moment of his death. With great generosity, Sheila Bender's writing shows how poetry can create moments when we can breathe, places where we can rest. Beyond that, fully aware of harsh losses, her work celebrates life, celebrates love.

—Peggy Shumaker, *Just Breathe Normally*

This is a story about the healing power of love and grief, written with an elegant simplicity and authenticity that is bound to touch anyone who reads it.

—Miriam Greenspan, *Healing Through the Dark Emotions: the Wisdom of Grief, Fear, and Despair*

Two pathways: the narrative of a life, a family, of intentions and love, of what was, what was to be, of what ends abruptly and the poetry, a doorway into unyielding grief and an opening for unique healing. The psychology in Bender's combined approach wisely and simply continues to un-layer and heal the grief.

—Dr. Linda L. Moore, *Release From Powerlessness: A Guide for Taking Charge of Your Life*

Sheila Bender writes poignantly about the Continental Divide in her life, the death of her son, Seth. I imagine the rivers of the past, when Seth was alive in the world, flowing east, and the rivers of the present flowing in the opposite direction, to the western land. Returning to reading and writing poetry in the midst of her grief, Bender searches for meaning in loss. Through poetry, she finds her new voice and discovers how to give form to what has no body. This moving and significant memoir demonstrates the deepening of art that sometimes follows loss. Poetry becomes the sun that lights what is, after all, a single country.

—Meg Files, *Write from Life*

A New Theology

Turning to Poetry in a Time of Grief

OTHER BOOKS BY SHEILA BENDER

Perfect Phrases for College Application Essays

Writing and Publishing Personal Essays

Writing Personal Essays:
How to Shape Your Life Experiences for the Page

Keeping a Journal You Love

A Year in the Life: Journaling for Self-Discovery

Writing Personal Poetry:
Creating Poems from Your Life Experiences

Sustenance: New and Selected Poems

The Writer's Journal:
40 Contemporary Writers and Their Journals

Writing in a New Convertible with the Top Down
(co-authored with Christi Killien)

Writing in a Convertible with the Top Down:
A Unique Guide for Writers
(co-authored with Christi Killien)

Love from the Coastal Route: Poems

Near the Light: Poems

A New Theology

TURNING TO POETRY IN A TIME OF GRIEF

Sheila Bender

Sheila Bender

Port Townsend, WA

10/10/13

IMAGO
P R E S S
TUCSON ARIZONA

Published in the United States of America by:

Imago Press
3710 East Edison
Tucson AZ 85716
www.imagobooks.com

Translations of Rainer Maria Rilke's *Duino Elegies* by Robert Hunter, copyright Hulogosi Cooperative Publishers, 1989. Used with Permission.

"One Art" from *The Complete Poems 1927-1979* by Elizabeth Bishop. Copyright © 1979, 1983 by Alice Helen Methfessel. Reprinted by permission of Farrar, Straus and Giroux, LLC.

Excerpt from Robert Desnos' poem, "The Voice of Robert Desnos," translated by William Kulik in the collection, *The Voice*. Used with Permission.

Library of Congress Cataloging-in-Publication Data
Bender, Sheila.
  A new theology : turning to poetry in a time of grief / Sheila Bender.
    p. cm.
  ISBN-13: 978-1-935437-04-8 (pbk. : alk. paper)
  ISBN-10: 1-935437-04-6 (pbk. : alk. paper)
  1. Grief. 2. Loss (Psychology) 3. Grief--Poetry. I. Title.
  BF575.G7B446 2009
  155.9'37092--dc22
                                        2009030952

Book Design by Leila Joiner
Cover photo: Sunrise from the Beach at the Port Townsend Marine
    Science Center by Kurt VanderSluis, 2009

ISBN 978-1-935437-04-8
ISBN 1-935437-04-6

Printed in the United States of America on Acid-Free Paper

ACKNOWLEDGMENTS

"Ashes" appeared in slightly different form in *Tiny Lights: A Journal of Personal Narrative*, Volume 9, Number 2, December 2003.

"I Call to the Slopes at Breckenridge" appears online in *The Psychoanalytic Experience: Analysands Speak*, an anthology of voices from the client's perspective, edited by Esther Helfgott at http://www.analysands.homestead.com/BenderCall.html and *Cascade* No. 1, Journal of the Washington Poet's Association Anthology.

"A New Theology" appeared in the *Bellingham Review*, Volume XXV, No. 2, Issue #51.

"I Remember Gold Lake" appeared in *Tidepools*, Spring, 2005.

"After We Collected Treasures from the Forests, 1977", "Burying the Dead Fish", "Poem of Sustenance", "After Crossing the Desert, 1983", "Rowing on Lake Union, 1978", "After a Great Love, 1983" (re-titled "After Love"), "Foggy Afternoon in Cambridge,1992", and "While Buying a Birthday Card for My Son Who's Just Gone to College" appear in *Sustenance: New and Selected Poems* by Sheila Bender, Fithian Press, Santa Barbara, 1999.

"Point Reyes, 1979", "Missing You", "If We, 1985", "Camping the Skykomish", and "And Now, 1987" appeared in *Love From the Coastal Route, Poems,* by Sheila Bender, Duckabush Press, Seattle, 1991.

"Sitting in the Black and Gold Replica of an Early American Rocker" and "Poetry" appeared in poetry columns in *Writer's Digest* magazine, 1998-1999.

WITH GRATITUDE

This book has taken seven years to write. Along the way, many friends, family members, and writing colleagues read my drafts with understanding, compassion, and the confidence that I could craft a book from my journey through grief. Among the many I thank for reading along the way are:

Meg Files

Christi Killien

Paula Jones Gardiner

Tracy Costigan

Fran Costigan

Emily Bender

Kurt VanderSluis

Marion Haber

Jan Halliday

Joy Johannessen

Nancy Levinson

Arline Lillian

Susan Bono

Stan Rubin

Caroline Arnold

Brenda Miller

Joanne Rocklin

Elizabeth Wales

Barbara Sjoholm

Jan Wright

Sara J. Glerum

Jandy Nelson

Ellie Matthews

Ruth Whitney

Janet Cox

Pat Simpson

Stephanie Reith

Judith Kitchen

Special thanks to Jeanne Yeasting for her detailed account of our experience at Gold Lake, to Michael Kane for his letter, and J. Michael Rona for his generous gift of the benches at the Port Townsend Science Center.

For my family and for all who mourn

List of Illustrations

TABLE OF CONTENTS

…only continuation

—Thich Nhat Hanh

BRETHREN

Tomorrow I head to Port Townsend for my friend Sheila's 60th birthday party. Already—like an athlete visualizing a complicated set of plays—I've gone through all the moves I must make: packing the car, getting the dog organized, stopping for food and flowers, the long, but not too long, ride to the tiny ferry terminal on an island, and the ferry that will take me to a peninsula, where I'll sit in the car with my dog, the first one on deck, so the water glistens multicolored all around us. I will drive along roads lined with tall trees until I reach her house overlooking a bay—the water, from this perspective, a calm sheen of blue. Her daughter will be there already, and her two grandsons, who look exactly like miniature men, and the Siamese cat, and her husband with his hearty laugh. And even her son will be there, though he died many years ago, because her son is always there. Not "by her side," exactly, but inside and emanating outward—his smile and his gaze infusing every room.

I will bustle inside, with my energetic dog taking the lead and my own ghosts crowding in behind, and I'll hug my friend, who is short and compact, so that when I hug her she fits right below my collarbone, and I know we'll exclaim at the joy of seeing one another again, because with her it is always as if we are coming home to one another, to a friendship that is not merely an idea of friendship, but a true dwelling place, with walls painted an earthy shade of gold, and clear windows that let in light in all weathers. I will remember (because I always remember) the time I entered this home a week after her son died and saw my friend in the chair by the window, heartache a new light illuminating that familiar face, a face that would now be forever changed. Her grief instantly became a shared grief, something that now lived within both of us, she was that porous. I offered my paltry gift—a picture frame, something to perhaps hold a memory—and though I didn't know what to say except Oh Sheila, I didn't have to say anything, it was all understood, all of it came out in the roundness of that Oh, an Oh like a mantra, an essential syllable of sorrow. I understood, then, that we would be friends for a long time, that grief can be a channel in which you swim alone, but where you can also find your brethren as they flicker along beside you, their bodies gliding in and out of focus in such deep and liquid light.

—Brenda Miller, author of *Blessing of the Animals*

PROLOGUE

The ancient Egyptians had a story in which a hero named Seth destroyed the dragon Apophis. It was thought that Apophis commanded an army of demons that plagued mankind. Every day, Apophis tried to devour the Sun Boat of Ra as it sailed the heavens. Seth's role was to battle Apophis and keep him from destroying the boat. Occasionally, however, Apophis succeeded, and the world was plunged into darkness. Seth and his companion, Mehen, cut a hole in Apophis's belly to allow the Sun Boat to escape. Only by putting faith in the gods of light could people defeat the demons.

CHAPTER ONE

Hey Dudes,
I hope you're
having as much fun
as me.
We are at Lakedale
campground on San-
Juan. My writing
is so bad because
I'm dodging bees.
The riding's been
pretty good (of course
I have the heaviest
load).

WP-769
SUNSET IN WASHINGTON
Typical scene in the San Juan Islands and Puget
Sound.   *Photo by Ed Cooper*   *Plastichrome*

POST CARD

Mukmort Bendersluis
128 N. 82nd
Seattle, WA
98103

Love,
Seth

FIRST

After We Collected Treasures from the Forests, 1977

I touch the cones of Douglas fir we brought
from the forests, bracts shaped like tails of mice
who ran up the tallest trees trying to hide from fire.
I think of you when you napped, hair wisps of smoke
against the amber linings of your sleeping bags.
Daughter, do you remember how you woke once
and told me in your dream you slit yourself
open and bled until a fairy came with magic dust
and a wand to heal your cut and teach you how to fly?
Son, when we walked in our alley looking for garden
snails on the undersides of leaves that hung over the fences,
did you notice dandelions and sheep's sorrel thriving,
making it possible for other plants to grow?

Curtains closed against the brightness of sunlight on snow. Respirator whooshing and clunking in the dim light. Seth's chest rising and falling to its rhythm. I cross the threshold of my son's Denver area hospital room quietly, as if trying not to wake him. Kristen, his fiancée, sits in a chair drawn up to his bedside, her thin frame curved over him like a question mark. Tears spill from her eyes as she massages his hand, letting him know she is there. The sparkle on the engagement ring he'd given her in the summer dips in and out of view as her fingers work his hand. I know she is trying to rub their connection, his spirit, back into him. Her mother, Jackie, rises to hug me, leaving the chair she's occupied all night. "I am so sorry this is happening to you."

"To us," I answer. We were to have been *mishpooka*, the Yiddish word for the group that becomes a family through marriage.

"I keep wishing I had asked Seth to spend the whole day yesterday downhill skiing with me," Kristen says quietly. "But I knew he wanted some time by himself on the slopes after all the family stuff we'd been doing…all the wedding shopping. We were so busy, and everyone was together for days. But I know he would have gone with me. Why didn't I insist?"

And I think of my boy needing space, getting it from the woman he loved. And I wish he hadn't needed it. I wish he had stuck with the group and done whatever they did. "Chill, Mom," he would say to me when I seemed too worried and too frantic about making everything work for everyone involved. But I am not trying to make anything work now. I have known for hours that Seth won't be waking up. His stepfather, Kurt, won't be teasing him about the goatee he hadn't told us about. I won't be making plans to stay with Seth until we can take him home. Kristen won't be describing her newly chosen wedding dress. Seth's sister, Emily, and her new husband, Vijay, won't be making dinner for all four of them again when they return to Northern California, won't be installing new software for Seth, fixing his computer compatibility problems, receiving his help on putting their computer desk together. My children's passions and skills were bringing them together again after years of them going off in different directions to different states. If only they had had more time.

Seth has slipped away from us, though the doctors are still waiting for an angiogram so they can be sure they are right that no blood has been getting to his brain since his snowboarding accident, when he went airborne on a Breckenridge slope and slammed headfirst into a tree. How is it I don't feel angry with my child for setting out without taking proper precautions, without renting and wearing a helmet? That I am not angry at everybody who was with him for not making him wear one? I know I am in shock, but the truth is I don't feel angry, and I am not full of blame. Seth is dead, and I have to honor my son. Anger will trivialize this day, make what I need to do impossible. Today, more than ever, my boy is an altar to which we bring our love. His shocking early death not a shock at all, exactly, but a finished poem, something "as it was first perceived to be, a thing always in existence," as Louise Gluck says of her finished poems. I am sure that I knew he would die young.

As far back as I can remember, since Seth was five, I felt I would lose him. I look at the fit, handsome poem of my boy lying in the bed and remember that Gluck says perceiving the existence of a poem as yet unwritten is to be "haunted by it; some sound, some tone, becomes a torment—the poem embodying that sound seems to exist somewhere already finished." I worried. I watched him grow. I celebrated and loved this boy, this young man. I tried to figure out which would be safer: mountain biking in the Tucson heat at the University of Arizona or skiing outside of Boulder if he attended the University of Colorado. I worried that he would stand too close to the edge of the Grand Canyon when he and a friend stopped on his way to his sister's UC Berkeley graduation. I worried the winter he went deep-sea fishing in Mexico with Kristen's father, Bob. My worry was a torment, something I knew already in existence, something I tried to tell myself was only normal, foolish, mother worrying.

And yesterday it happened. The snow at Breckenridge melted just a little while Seth was eating lunch with Kristen and her family. When he returned for a last run, the melt had frozen over. And then, after no deaths all season on the slopes at Breckenridge, helmet or no, three people died in separate areas. And one of them was Seth, though the doctors were not quite letting go of him yet.

A social worker asks if Emily and Vijay would like to speak with her. I stand there, listening to the respirator's whoosh, and examine my boy, feel his skin, take in how beautiful he is. I do not know how long I stand there. I do not think about saying goodbye. Kurt knows I have a terrible headache, and he has gone looking for Tylenol.

Seventeen hours ago, when all of our lives were changing, I was on a writing holiday. I'd left my study, my cell phone, and my manuscript for an uninterrupted tea with writer friends I didn't often see. I returned to my writing house in the early winter dusk. Everything was still except for the persistent red pulse of a message light. I pushed the button and heard a man identify himself as chaplain at the hospital where my son had been helicoptered. At the words "accident on the Breckenridge slopes" and "coma," I stood paralyzed, hardly able to move my fingers to write down the number to return his call. As I dialed, my anxiety turned to motion. I paced between the kitchen counter and the dining table, thinking this was a close call but not the final poem, only a draft with a different ending, one that would buy more time. What to take to stay in Denver until Seth wakes up from his coma? How would he wake up? Functioning? Would there be a wedding in June? When the chaplain answered, he said doctors were still working on Seth; he said Seth's dad, Jim, was on his way; he said he thought I might want to come, too.

Might want to come? Why would he think I needed to be told to come? I begged the chaplain to connect me to a doctor or a nurse, but he said there was no one available to tell me more. I dialed Jim's cell phone and caught him on the airport concourse. He told me doctors had put a shunt in to help drain fluid from our son's swollen brain. He told me there was only a small chance that Seth would survive. I called Kristen's cell phone, and she spoke to me from the car her father was driving to the hospital where Seth had been helicoptered after the ski patrol found him.

"I'll be out there as soon as I can get on a plane, Kristen. We'll get him well. There will be a wedding," I said hopefully.

"I don't know," came the reply in a wavering voice.

I had never heard Kristen sound uncertain.

I called Emily and Vijay, who were visiting in Seattle, and Kurt at work in Los Angeles. He wasn't there. His cell was off. Emily and Vijay would keep trying him while I took the ferry to Seattle. Vijay booked us on the first plane out in the morning. Kurt would book his flight to Denver, I thought, as I hurried to pack so I could cross Puget Sound. But when I opened drawers, I couldn't focus on what I needed. I thought to just get into the car and drive to the ferry without the clothes, but I couldn't stop shaking. I ran to my neighbor's. At 4 PM, Discovery Bay, one short block from our houses, was the color of ghosts.

"Seth is unconscious in a hospital in Denver. He was airlifted there. He had a snowboarding accident. Jim said he went at high speed into a tree. I can't get anything packed." Ashen, Judy walked back to my house with me and packed me a suitcase with warm clothes, while I paced and nodded my agreement with what she was folding for me. Then she and her husband drove me the hour to the Seattle ferry. Emily and Vijay met me on the Seattle side and brought me to my parents' house, where they had been visiting while they were up from California.

My father's advanced Parkinson's had slowed my parents down considerably. It was a treat for them to have Emily and her husband of six months as overnight guests. So, although she and Vijay had settled at Jim's as home base for their trip, they had brought a small suitcase to my folks'. It sat unopened.

What does a mother remember from the hours she is waiting to see her son, almost surely dead of a brain injury? The mattresses of her mother's trundle daybed made up with matching sheets, and the welcoming glow of a small bedside lamp in the guest room. The lingering smell of pot roast from dinner, same as during childhood, when better parents than I kept their children safe.

When I did reach Kurt, who'd been at a company Christmas movie treat and dinner, he insisted that he'd come to meet us in a few days.

"A few days?" I shrieked. "Even though they're saying there's very little likelihood he'll survive?"

Kurt was adamant. His response to this shocking news was to say that he would finish his workweek, and then join me. He probably focused on being the one who would bring fresh energy to our bedside vigil. He wasn't one to think he could help when doctors were already there. But Kurt hadn't spoken to Jim, hadn't heard the quiver in Kristen's voice. He didn't seem to be hearing how much I needed him to be with me; no need was greater at the moment than his need to deny the likely loss of Seth. If he were only right, I thought.

Too tired to argue or plead, too sad to deal with resistance, I returned to what I needed to get through the night. I told my mother I'd have to sleep at Jim's with Emily and Vijay, so we could all leave for the airport together at 5:30 in the morning.

"Why? You can all stay here," she said. "There's room. It's late."

But Emily and Vijay needed to return to Jim's to pack clothes to take with them, and they didn't want to cross the I-90 floating bridge twice before early morning. Although their reasoning made sense, neither my mother nor I was clinging to logic. Emily was the closest thing I had to Seth, and I was clinging to her. My mother was clinging to us, too. And my dear father, unable to speak much or sit for too long, had had to go to bed. He'd never been one to talk about tragedy. He'd always just gone on. Seth was his only grandson, a boy he could joyfully share the male world with after raising two girls. I wondered if my dad might be thinking like Kurt—that we would all bring a recuperating Seth home after some days in the hospital. He'd never had to say much to me about unhappy things except, "It's not that bad. You'll live," because it was always true. Perhaps, in his mind, this would just have to be that way.

Jim's wife, Ann, laid aside the knitting she was doing to keep herself occupied while she waited to hear more from Jim. Exhausted, or maybe feeling the strangeness of having me sleep in her dad's house, Emily pointed me in the direction of the room that had been made for her when she and Seth lived part of each week at each parent's house. In the dark, I couldn't find the light switch for the room, but from the light of a small fixture in the hallway I could see that Ann was forcing bulbs in the room. Newspapers covered clay pots. I felt for the bed and, as I lay down in my clothes, I made a pact with myself to glance at the newspapers first thing in the morning; whatever words my eyes fell upon would prepare me for the coming day's events.

Eventually, I fell into a fitful sleep, and when Emily put on the light and woke me to get ready, I looked in the direction of the papers. The heavy type read: Obituaries. On our way to the airport, my cell phone rang. Kurt was already at LAX and ready to board. He had rented a car at the Denver airport. He would pick us up outside of luggage.

Adjusting her sweater over her shoulders, Jackie curses the family decision not to take a warm weather vacation. Me, too, though I do not know if it would have made a difference in the drafting of Seth's life poem. I do know that, although we are Jewish, Seth enjoyed Christmas gatherings with Kristen's family, and each year for three years he loved joining them in Kansas City on Christmas eve and, the day after Christmas, flying with them for a week's vacation. This year, Jackie had decided they would not to go to Hawaii so she and Kristen and Seth would have time, after being away, to make wedding preparations before the kids returned to Berkeley for Seth's work and Kristen's graduate architecture studies.

The queasy feeling I'd had when Seth first told us about Kristen's family vacations each winter, and how he'd be going with them, overcomes me now. I had told myself that the feeling I'd had the day he told us was mere jealousy—after all, Seth was saying that he'd be away from his family over the holidays each year on a glamorous trip. But it hadn't really felt like jealousy—ever since my divorce from Jim, Thanksgiving was the holiday I spent with my kids, and Christmas was the one they spent with him. I wouldn't be forfeiting the holiday Seth spent with me. The feeling I had was worry, fear that something would happen to Seth, something beyond anyone's control while he was on one of those trips. Still, I tried on the idea that the feeling was part of some mothering neurosis, like taking to heart the thinking that, with Seth's serious attachment to Kristen, I was losing a son, while her family was gaining one. But I knew I was gaining a daughter. And now she is right here in this hospital room, tears slipping continuously down her cheeks.

I pull the collar of my fleece vest over my mouth, hoping the moisture in my breath will wash over me, soothe my aching head. Kurt brings me the Tylenol he's found, and we leave to find some water. We see Jim by the grey metal elevator doors.

"I've just talked with the doctors. They still want to do the angiogram. His brain is bruised and so swollen that blood is probably unable to move into it."

I glance at the notebook Jim is holding. "I spent the night writing things down, 'Seth style,'" he said. I love the way Jim names his memories of Seth's way in the world. I see my own pain in Jim's, and I let tears form for the first time since I heard about the accident. Jim is doing all he can to breathe his eldest son alive by getting our boy down on the page: Seth cooking and baking and flying kites. Seth sailing.

I immediately start a list of images. First summer: Seth building a kayak. Seth sitting on the deck in the sun with a cup of coffee, enraptured with the world. Seth showing me the black Northwest Native American orca totem he has chosen to paint on the bow of his kayak. And then images from fall: four-year-old Seth puzzling out the way he should be older than his sister because each year his October birthday comes before her birthday nine days later. Twenty-year-old Seth brewing beer with his college friends and making sure the bottles and apparatus are properly disinfected. Now spring: Twenty-five-year-old Seth figuring out how to build a *chupa* out of bamboo poles, the canopy his sister and her groom stood under during their wedding ceremony. No winter memories right now, only the real event we are living through. And then I remember one: Seth walking the five miles from his dad's house to my house when I lived in Seattle. A surprise snowfall stopped all buses the first winter holiday he came home from school in Boulder. Bundled now, as all Colorado mountain boys, in wool cap and gloves and flannel shirt, he made his way over the Fremont Bridge. A talent scout for a Coors beer commercial stopped him and suggested he audition. But he wasn't yet twenty-one, so there was no chance he could. Still, the moment charmed him, and he charmed us recounting it.

A hodgepodge of years fill my mind. At fourteen, Seth saying, "If only I can get that first job." My amazement at the seriousness with which he took growing up. Within a month, he was bussing tables at a French restaurant every Friday night and Saturday, handsome in his black pants and white shirt. When he took his driver's test at sixteen, he scored 100 percent, not only on the written exam but also on the driving part, unheard of for new drivers. Standing square-shouldered and handsome before me in front of our stained glass kitchen window, he told me there were no rules I could make that he couldn't now break, so I'd have to trust him and realize I'd raised him well, which, he said, I did.

A year later, he designed the Port Townsend writing retreat I wanted to build. When we fought over bathroom fixture decisions that led to redrawing the bathroom plans in a way he didn't like, I assured him that, someday, he'd realize I wasn't the client from hell. I never told him I also believed he'd someday thank me for the opportunity to design a house he'd see built before he finished his freshman year of college. I thought he might get around to thanking me when he was forty, but his first year in the University of Colorado's pre-architecture program he told me he understood what an opportunity I'd given him. He presented me with a rendering of the house, the subject he chose for a college class assignment.

All I can see is perfection in Seth and in his life: in the way he needed to live his life deeply and with emotional acceleration. We all felt that about him. I watch Emily and Vijay walk together down the hall from the hospital social worker's office, and I remember my daughter at four, after she'd fallen off a porch railing and been unconscious and suffered a concussion. I knew she was seriously hurt, but I never felt I would lose her. "I feel a little bit fine," she said, when the doctors asked her to stand up. Looking at Emily now, I realize she always demonstrates an outlook of "working with what you have." I am looking at less than a third of my son's life expectancy and trying to see it as a perfect life. It makes me a little bit fine.

When the resident and medical staff show up in their green scrubs to do the test, we wait in family rooms down the hall.

Kristen is with Kurt and me, and she tells us how she waited for Seth at a snack shop at the end of the run, so they could go back to her family's condo together. When he didn't show up, she contacted the ski patrol and found out they'd found him, provided CPR, and arranged to have him on life support as he was airlifted from the slope to the Denver hospital. Her family raced from their vacation condo in two rental cars. She thinks the hospital must have reached Jim with an emergency number Seth kept in his wallet, and that Jim had let the hospital know my number because, as her family drove, Jim reached them with more information than the ski patrol had given to them.

As we wait for the test results, I call my sister, my mother, my close friends. I need to be grounded in my larger community, and they need to know they are connected. There isn't much to say, so our conversations are short. "We are still waiting." For some, I add that I've known from the moment I walked into the darkened hospital room that Seth is not in his body. "He is very far away," I say to those I think will understand.

I walk into the room again and again to look at the body of my boy, slowly, the way I did the day he was born, memorizing it all: his comfortable, medium height, surprisingly large, wide feet, his broad fingernails, their bright moons, the very tight curl in his light brown hair. Broad shoulders, very lean from daily bike rides between North Berkeley and his office at a downtown Oakland architecture firm, sun-bleached hair on his chest and arms from California hiking and camping, sapphire eyes I can't see now beneath his closed lids.

A nervous resident returns to tell us conclusively that no blood has gotten to Seth's brain since the time of impact, when his brain had immediately swelled inside his skull. He offers us science to document what we already know, to give us a way to never feel that we should have kept life support going.

The social worker asks if we'd like a rabbi to come and, though neither Jim nor I is observant, I say I'd like that. I want to hear the sounds of ancient prayers, the sound of words laden with centuries of grief.

The rabbi comes quickly and leads us in prayers, as both families hold hands around Seth's bed. When the rabbi finishes, all of us stay very still, encircling Seth. I had never before had to do anything at the close of these prayers. The dead they were said for had never been in the room with me. Since I have asked for the rabbi, the others in the room must think that I know what to do. They seem to be waiting for me to lead them. Or perhaps it is respect for me as Seth's mother. Slowly, I walk forward and bend over the bedrail to kiss Seth's cheek, to touch his skin for the last time. I try not to disturb the respirator tubes and wires. I do not want to feel clumsy next to my son, who was always so careful, so aware of his surroundings, so attentive to any task he was doing. This time, I take in the way his right eye is black from blood draining in his skull.

It is the second time I'd seen him with a black eye. When he was in eighth grade, Kurt and I picked him up on one of his first evenings as a busboy. I noticed he had a black eye as he entered our car. After he took his seat in the back, I asked him about it. At school that day, he had refused to pick up a piece of paper a classmate dropped, and the classmate punched him and slammed him against the lockers. Maybe he had had a small concussion, the school nurse told him, but Seth didn't call us because he wanted to go to work. That job was so important to him.

"My boy," I say aloud at his hospital bedside. In the days ahead, I'll repeat the words, and more images of Seth will flood over me. Seth waist high in a trench he was digging when he was an undergraduate studying architecture, and his uncle had gotten him a construction job to gain hands-on building experience. Kurt and I listening to jazz on the radio as we waited in the dark for Seth's junior high ski bus to arrive from the mountains on Saturday nights, excited kids disembarking with their gear, creating a sudden eddy in the parking lot. Grade school-aged Seth on the city pier in winter, when he'd urged Kurt and me to take him squid fishing, so he could show us what Jim had taught him about watching for a sudden luminescence flowing in with the night tide. Seth at twenty-five again in front of me, hair trimmed for his professional architecture job, that goatee started.

I see Kurt on the other side of the bed, staring at the boy he'd helped raise from age nine, the high schooler he'd discussed sex with for a health class assignment, the grade school child whose train set he had admired, noticing that the thrill for Seth was not the train on its tracks, but the buildings he had made for the train to run past.

"My boy. My young man. My boy." I kiss his cheek again and feel how cool his body is, without the warmth of my child, who ran hot in any season. I don't want to move from his side. I want to hear him loving us, hear his voice, as I did when he asked so politely whether having his wedding celebration at a rustic resort in Colorado would be okay with us and whether hanging out with the whole blended family in that setting would feel all right. "How could it not?" Kurt and I told him. "We are your team, the people rooting for you at all times."

"We're here, baby, and it's not a grade school teacher's conference or a school play. We're here at your deathbed," I whisper to myself, not believing my own words. "Your team."

I move back into the circle to let the others take their turns kissing my boy. Jim comes next to Seth's side. He lowers the bedrail easily, a motion I read as "we need no barriers" and says what he needs to, then the others take their turns, all of us trying to believe as best we can that we will never see Seth breathing, even artificially, again.

CHAPTER TWO

HOME

Burying the Dead Fish, 1981

In the sink the gills open again
like flesh from a wound. My son
and I stand in the flat stare
of this fish without breath.
In the light of a waning moon
he buries this small life carefully
under sunflowers moldy with fall.
Feel of earth, feel of death,
he does this with his hands knowing
each loss wants a marker.
How can he bury a marriage that died?
Loving both parents wasn't enough
to keep them together. The distance
between being alive and going back
to being dead becomes pain and he holds it,
a salmon in the rivers of his spawning.

In the morning, Jim flies home to his wife and sons in Seattle. Emily and Vijay go with him to help prepare for the funeral services, which I have requested be conducted very soon, as is Jewish custom. It is imperative to me that we follow through, that we continue on the course of this finality, that we hang together in this time outside of time, rather than scatter and remain too long in our own respective geographical areas. Kristen's family heads to Kansas City to ready themselves for the trip to Seattle and Seth's funeral. After everyone leaves the Denver hotel, Kurt and I drive to my cousin Marion's nearby house, where we will stay while we wait for the mortuary to release Seth's ashes.

At night, sitting side by side at a little table in Marion's finished basement, we type on our laptop to friends and family, telling them our awful news. So trained are my fingers that they rhythmically tap out words on the keyboard as if nothing unusual has happened. But putting a title on the memo going out to so many who will be shocked makes me pause. I don't know if it is okay to use email to convey this news, but I certainly can't face calling so many friends and relatives and colleagues. I type, "Very sad news about Seth Bender" in the memo subject line and hold my breath. Will the recipients guess what is coming in the body of the message? Will the subject title soften the shock of what comes next? Will it help that they will wonder how sad "sad" might be before they read that Seth is not just in a hospital after a horrible accident? I can't type "Seth Bender is Dead" in the subject line. I have to give people the chance to hesitate before they read on and find this out, a moment to prepare in some way for the words, "Seth died."

As we click addresses from our address book onto the email, we receive a draft of an obituary Jim and Emily wrote on their plane ride to Seattle. I haven't yet thought of all the kinds of writing required when death comes. Kurt and I recognize some of what Jim had written in his notebook as he sat the whole night by Seth's bedside, along with Kristen and Jackie. We add a thought Kurt has about donations mourners might make in Seth's name to the Port Townsend Marine Science Center, a community resource that Seth had used as the subject of his architecture master's thesis.

Although my fingers are typing, I am not fully imagining that this is going to be published the next day in the Seattle newspapers. Email to friends and family is one thing, but a newspaper obituary makes Seth's death public and archival, more permanent than I can imagine even in this very moment of telling people I know. The mind doesn't work very thoroughly in shock. I forget to add my parents to the list of family who survive Seth. Putting myself among the survivors was surreal enough. How could he be gone before his grandparents? Informing people about Kurt's donation idea made the obituary seem, for a moment, more like a newsletter article about the living.

Two days later, Kurt and I arrive in Port Townsend. As the short daylight turns to dusk, we begin writing about Seth for a eulogy. This time, as we write, an email arrives from Kurt's father in Michigan, with fond memories of Seth as a preteen playing host to his grand-steppies, as he called Kurt's folks. As we sit at my desk by our window overlooking Discovery Bay, we write his father's memories into our eulogy and plan to read the eulogy at services standing together, alternating paragraphs. Being near each other will help us get through this task we want more than anything to do well. The only thing that feels soothing now, after we've said goodbye to Seth, is talking and writing and reading about him.

That night our bed is shaking, and it wakes me up. There is no earthquake. Our cat, who sometimes stretches against the mattress and makes vibrations, is in Los Angeles, not up here with us. I like to think Seth has come by to let me know he's here.

At the funeral, Emily is the first called by the rabbi to the bema, the front of the synagogue where the podium stands. She stands alone and reads her words about what being her brother's sister meant to her from childhood to young adulthood, how accepted she felt finally by the young architect, who, as a child, had frequently made fun of her scholarly passion.

"When Seth and I were little, we were teammates," she says. "We went back and forth together between Mom's house and Dad's house. Our lives were split between two places and two families, but we made the transitions together, so Seth was the core of my family, the only one who shared my whole situation, who was always there. We fought like siblings do, but we also hung together."

She learned how to have a long distance relationship when Vijay was her fiancé, and they lived on different coasts, or sometimes even different countries. She knew how to keep a relationship going over distances, and she isn't going to lose her relationship with Seth. She will make sure it endures, she says firmly. The curls in her blonde hair, always a touch lighter than the curls in his hair, sway as she nods. So far, she has always been able to achieve what she's imagined. When she wanted to study in France her junior year of high school, she turned down an opportunity to go to French-speaking Africa when she hadn't been chosen for France. She stayed on the waiting list and, within weeks, a small town in the Southeast of France lost their exchange student, and she was in. When she wanted to spend a college year in Japan, a place became available at a university in Sendai.

I know my daughter's determination. I know her focus. I know the way the world comes through for her. And I know that, if the long distance relationship she wants with Seth is possible, she'll sustain it. But how acutely I feel the absence of her little brother, who'd been in the audience when his sister gave speeches as a two-time Valedictorian. Smiling, he never revealed if he still felt as he had when he was in elementary school: *Emily's reading is making me bored. I want her to play with me.* How unpaired she looks up there, Emily without Seth.

The rabbi reads words that Jim and Ann are too emotional to read. Ann's first: "I met Seth when he was five," Ann has written. "I called him my 'Honey Boy.' They said he wouldn't give hugs and kisses, so I gave him mine. I remember driving him to work at the QFC in the snow; he was in his short sleeves. I remember him thanking us in college for not letting him have a Nintendo in the house."

Then Jim's: "As an architect, Seth drew straight lines. He also knew that enough straight lines connected together form a strong circle. We are finding great comfort in the circles of our friends and family who are gathering around us. Seth's energy, spirit, and love have touched many people. We are so pleased to hear your memories and see photos of Seth and to learn about him through your eyes."

Next, Kristen and her father stand together while Kristen reads about meeting Seth at college, and Bob tells of the way Kristen came home one semester saying, "Seth says," before everything she related. Her dad wondered how a young guy could be so quotable. And then he met Seth and found himself also starting sentences with the words, "Seth said." I smile. I'd heard Kurt do the same thing. Emily and me, too.

When Kurt and I rise to read our eulogy, we look out over 350 friends and family, listening through their tears. We take over for one another whenever our own tears keep our tongues from working.

Kurt: "In Walnut Creek, California a couple years ago, Seth and I, who are not cigar smokers, bought wonderful cigars one night and walked around the city. Having the cigars in our hands slowed the world down to the speed where I could really notice the things that Seth always took in. Walnut Creek had created a pedestrian space that was inviting and useful. Seth explained to me how it worked and the decisions that were made to make me feel the way I felt—decisions about how high the lamps were and how close they were to the curb, the width of the sidewalk and the height of the façade, and the spacing between the park benches."

Sheila: "There were many times when Seth let others see the world through his eyes. At twelve, Seth introduced Kurt's parents to Seattle one afternoon. We had given him the assignment of accompanying them downtown and entertaining them. Gen and Ade remember a curly-headed bundle of energy giving them directions to The Pike Place Market and the aquarium and back home again."

Kurt: "When Sheila and I didn't make it home from a meeting by dinner, Seth prepared the three of them a pasta meal. They fell in love with this young man, who looked after two elderly people he had never seen before with care and attention. They loved watching him dribble a basketball while skateboarding to the school grounds to shoot baskets and listening to him name each fish in his aquarium and explain their backgrounds. They enjoyed the way he referred to the bicycle he rode all over town for the latest gadgetry as his 'wheels,' and they listened as he spoke about all the accessories he had for his plaster-cracking stereo and how they all worked together."

Sheila: "Once, Seth and I hiked in Rocky Mountain National Park, the aspen leaves clapping in the breeze. As we sat down to a picnic of goat cheese and sourdough bread, he told me the philosophy he had worked out with a friend when they biked Eldorado Canyon—it was that life is all about 'food' and 'stuff,' how the amount of food and stuff you need to appreciate your life and live well is not all that big if you choose the right stuff and the right food.

"That day in the Rockies, Seth also told me the aspen is the largest known organism in the world, a whole stand one tree. I know I must come to understand that having and letting go is also one tree. I must believe I have the right stuff and the right food to appreciate my life and my son for the rest of my days."

We sit back down in the front row of the synagogue's sanctuary, sadder than before we read. But it helps, somehow, to think that everyone with us is a shimmering leaf.

The rabbi closes the service by reading one of my poems, as Kurt had asked him to:

Poem of Sustenance

This is the poem that stands
in the moonlight singing,
that rises from sleep
because in darkness stars
are seen, because in darkness
you see what you will
and in darkness you dream.
And when fear washes
you away and the moon
is a cold light vanishing,
this is the poem that swims
among the coral casting
its net for the small
yellow fish or the stars.

As he listens, Kurt sobs next to me. I feel the community
of people, who had known Seth, sobbing. His teachers from
elementary school and junior high are there behind me. Parents
are there with their kids who were Seth's schoolmates. Neigh-
bors from all the streets his dad and I had ever collectively
lived on in Seattle are there. Ex-lovers of mine and high school
sweethearts of Seth's sit in the sanctuary. Cousins and aunts
and uncles from Seattle, the East Coast, and the middle of the
country anchor the room. My mother is beside my frail father,
his caretaker, and friends of theirs. Seth and Kristen's friends
from Berkeley and Colorado arrived by car when they couldn't
get flights during the busy holiday season. College roommates
of mine gathered, and a pastry chef who used to come to my
house to work on his poems has brought the pink bakery box

full of treats he always brought for my kids. Seth's bosses from the architecture firm where he worked in Oakland are there. In the darkest of all my days, everyone in the sanctuary is supplying the small yellow fish and the stars, Seth's light, and everything that reflects the eternal.

But, as much as our relationships to Seth reconstruct him, Seth is gone. Lines of poetry about death run through my head. Some are by Richard Blessing, one of my graduate school professors, who died from a brain tumor. Anticipating death, he wrote:

> ...not like entering a mirror nor like closing a door
> nor like going to sleep in a hammock of bones.
> You may expect what you like. It is nothing like that.

What was it like now for my son? I think of more lines by my professor:

> What will you be but the roof of your house
> and the voiceless stones of the house
> and the rain falling, harmless, beautiful,
> falling forever on the roof of the house?

From the day of Seth's services and for many weeks, people remain dedicated to not losing him. It rains letters and pictures and email notes from Jim and Ann, from Jackie, from Seth's friends, from my friends, from Seth's colleagues and his dad's, showing me more and more about Seth. I am not interested in much besides this resurrection of my son. If I am not reading these notes and looking at pictures of Seth, I am watching the sun rise or set. Hours go by without me.

At home again in Los Angeles, I hang pictures of Seth at different ages and many of his cards and notes to me on the walls of my house. I want only to stare at my son. Thankfully, the emails, notes, letters, and pictures keep coming from the people emotionally gathered around us despite great distances. I want nothing but to take in their memories of Seth:

"Every day at three, when Seth came home from his construction job, he glanced through our open door and saw me nursing my new baby. He always waved hello before he went in. Always."

"We were remodeling our house, and he would come over and check on the progress. The roof over the ceiling of our new bedroom was problematic for the architect, the framer, and my husband. Seth kept looking up at it, making suggestions, checking back to see what was going on with it."

"When he would explain his reasoning, you could see his maturity. His eyes were steady and his voice confident. He was a scholar among scholars. He could talk about the latest trends and theories. He knew how to design in steel, concrete, and glass. But it was Seth's belief in the informal axis, in wood, that I found so appealing. Seth believed in humanity and nature. He drew deep inspiration from who he was, his family and his values. Each piece of wood is unique in grain and color. It is the material of the Bay Area and the Pacific Northwest."

"No matter how intense and demanding his schedule, Seth always had this effortless sense of calm and equanimity about him. His drawing pencils were always neatly lined up on his desk with such a look of tranquility. And he always made time to think of and do for those he loved and for good food and fun."

"I remember his joy at designing the railings for my porch, like the ones for your house in Port Townsend of which he was so proud."

"Seth was my favorite roommate (sorry, Ted, Mike, and Davis) because he, more than anyone else, showed me how life was good. (You have to know how Seth would say "good," which I hear sometimes echoed in conversations with people close to me now who never had the pleasure of meeting Seth.)"

"Seth had an uncanny ability to give energy to situations as they arose around the house so that later he wouldn't need to deal with the same things over and over again."

"Late one night in studio, Seth and I got to talking about architecture and ecology and, sooner than we knew it, we were deep in conversation about life and the world at large, about caring for all people and the needs of those who don't have green places to go to."

Despite my aspen metaphor in the eulogy, despite my words about the tree of life being composed of having and letting go, despite knowing the small yellow fish and the stars are there, I have no idea about how to let go. I know how to want my son, to see him smile, marry his fiancée, pursue his career as an architect and father his children.

Without these possibilities, daily life doesn't seem at all right or even possible. I don't want to cook or shop for food. Going out to eat when Kurt and I try is painful. The laughter and bustle of others in the restaurant thrusts our pain into giant relief; we can't talk to each other the way the other diners do or feel comfortable with our silences the way we can at home. Kurt begins stopping on his way home to pick up take-out food for us. Being with friends whom we'd only so recently introduced to Seth on his visits to Los Angeles is nearly impossible. Sex seems like a violation. It is as if my body can't perform or enjoy itself. Drinking red wine at night after dinner helps in a way that food does not.

One day, walking past an antique store, I notice a lighting fixture and form an attachment to it. I go in and buy it for over our dining room table, because I associate Seth with dining room fixtures. When he was in college and home on vacation, he chose one for our Port Townsend house and hung it. He told me that the one he'd picked was the best he could do, given the budget I had allowed him. The one I pick now catapults me back.

While Kurt is at work, I watch the man who owns the antique shop install the lighting fixture for me. Watching him reminds me of Seth. Strangers are sometimes better company than the people I know. Anything I do that reminds me of times with Seth is real life. All other aspects of my life seem false and insignificant. If I do go to the grocery store, I go only to remember Seth: the way he hated the Lucky's in our neighborhood with its orange floor and its constant messages about saving money written on each aisle's linoleum. If I go to the bank, I go only because it is a branch of the one where I'd opened a free checking account with Seth when he was in high school because, with my name on it, I could put money in directly when he was in college. If I drive anywhere, it is only to remember Seth when he shopped for his first car and came home with an old brown Audi sedan, which we all felt was perfect and, of course, cost no more than I had allotted.

I can't concentrate on much outside of my memories, so I really don't know why I decide to keep my commitment to teach at the Southwest Society of Authors' conference. Maybe I am eager to see colleagues who had never met my children or discussed them. Perhaps I think I will be able to let go if I experience myself in that milieu. I fly to Tucson, Arizona, and each day I am at the conference I listen to other people's writing, with pain growing in the center of my chest. My grief seems to heighten toward afternoon. Is this because that's the time of day the hospital called to say my son was in a coma? Is it because at that time of day my body just runs out of what little energy grief allows me to crawl out of a well of suffering?

During a one-on-one session at the conference, a woman who doesn't know my situation brings a poem she has written for her friend, whose son died many years before. The poem is in the voice of the dead son speaking to his mother about his need for her to go on with her life. The son is saying that he can't do what is necessary until his mother is okay. I burst into tears as this poet tells me she doesn't feel that she can show this poem to her friend, who, many years since the boy died, still remains unavailable to those who love her and unavailable to live her life. This writer believes that her friend's son would not have wanted it this way. I tell her my grief. She is embarrassed to have brought me this poem. But I am glad to have read her poem; I am tired of keeping my feelings in the background as I teach. I hope she sees that, although she couldn't show her friend the poem, there are others who will benefit from reading it.

Thankfully, this one-on-one conference is the last of the day, and I return to my hotel room. I think about how I don't want to talk about much of anything most of the time. When my daughter calls almost daily, I hide this as I encourage her in her grief work and listen to her encouraging me.

Now that I have tried returning to my professional life, I realize I don't know where Emily is finding the energy to continue with her duties as a young professor, visit with Kristen, and attend a grief support group with her, as well as communicate so often with her dad and with me. My admiration for my daughter usually feeds my energy. But now that I have given up on escaping through professional life, I feel liked an abandoned barn. I don't really understand how my family continues without Seth. I don't know how I can.

When my daughter shares her dreams about Seth, however, my interest is piqued; it is as if each dream is actually news of him. Early on, she dreamt that Seth came to see her, and she asked him how it felt, dying. He told her he had fallen down, and when he got up he was surprised it was without his body. He appeared perplexed, but okay. Emily described a second dream:

"I felt like I was looking through a telescope. I think Seth was showing me what he was seeing. At first, there was a sun-splashed formal garden with a fountain and very structured bushes. We were seeing it from above. There were people in the garden, all wearing pastel-colored robes and floating. I couldn't see Seth because I was seeing what he was seeing. I said to him, 'This seems very clichéd,' and we moved to a different place. That place was inside, and there wasn't anyone there. It was dark and hard to focus on, and I think the ceiling had lots of arches. I said, 'I hope this isn't where you end up if you don't like the clichéd version.' We moved again. This time, what I saw was a big starscape, with all of the stars very clear, and then the stars all turned into fishes. What I figured from that last shift was that Seth is in a place that can be whatever he wants it to be, like he's in the best possible place for an architect because he can design a space and be in it right away."

I immediately note that the images of fish and stars from my poem were in my daughter's dream, mixing one into the other. Is there a common source in what the unconscious knows, or had my writing, which she'd read and then heard the rabbi read, merely influenced her? Wondering about things like this has always made me begin poems, but I haven't had the desire or the concentration to write anything since the eulogy.

I sit alone in my Tucson hotel room with the recurring late afternoon ache in my chest. I think about the conference attendee's poem. Three weeks after he died, I imagine Seth telling me again what he'd told me at five: "I am making you a house on wheels, Mom, so you can write while I drive you around and around." Thinking about my daughter's dream, I know where Seth and I will be driving: I have to find a route to understanding the spirituality of death. Without that journey, I will be of no use to anyone.

CHAPTER THREE

ASHES

After Crossing the Desert, 1983

How the magpies taking off as we drive by
resemble pinwheels, I think aloud traveling
17 North between Othello and Moses Lake.
Then, a sign for Pasco where my sister's
in-laws farm alfalfa, asparagus.
I think about the half owners of the farm,
the uncle and the aunt who died last year,
killed by someone speeding through.
I hope to leave this planet gracefully
without the twisted metal, broken glass, gas
bursting into flame, without the fear I felt
an hour ago watching my son at the very edge of rock,
imagining his small body a blunt ax cutting
the long log of air between the cliffs and the Columbia.
I hope we leave forever upward, pin wheeling
the white on our wings, swirling and swirling
against that open, blue sky.

Every day I look at the picture Kurt took the first time we scattered Seth's ashes.

Feldman Brothers' mortuary called us at Marion's house two days after Seth's death to say we could come to get his ashes. Kurt and I had the idea of taking some to Gold Mountain Resort, two hours away in the mountains above Boulder, where Seth and Kristen were to have been married. Kurt called Kristen in Kansas City to find out what she thought. Tearful, but pleased, she told us how to find the outdoor site where she and Seth had decided to have their ceremony.

We also had the idea of stopping in Boulder to find our friend, Jeanne, who had known Seth since he was six. At the outskirts of town, we stopped at a local convenience store and asked the clerk for directions to nearby Forest Service cottages, where we knew she'd recently found temporary housing. Once at the cottage site in the forest, we saw an office. One employee was at her desk in the slow season just before New Year's. She told us which cottage was Jeanne's.

We walked past a rusting propane tank on the ground beside the cottage, pulled open a worn screen door and knocked. We took in the delight on Jeanne's face as she exclaimed, "What are you two doing here?" and took deep breaths before we told her the unbelievable news about where we were going. We watched her happy smile turn to a look of despair. Kurt and I waited on a low couch, our feet on the linoleum floor near her wood-burning stove, as she hurried to dress in warm clothes to come with us to spread Seth's ashes. She wasn't very far along the road of mourning her father's death. With her family, she had followed his wishes and cast his ashes into San Francisco Bay. After she had returned home, a hawk circled low in the sky above her for days while she gardened, and it felt to her like her father's spirit visiting.

With the box of Seth's ashes by my feet on the passenger side of the car, I realized that I wanted to take pictures of the wedding site, so we stopped again to buy a disposable camera. One hour outside of Denver, snow was falling over aspens. When Seth was a student in Colorado, we had visited him here and hiked this forest. We sat on rock ledges in spring and in fall, quiet and dwarfed, overlooking the Continental Divide, feeling overwhelmed by the majesty we were viewing. My life was now a Continental Divide. One continent with Seth on the earth with me; the other one without him here.

One more hour of driving, and Jeanne, Kurt, and I spotted a patch of silver grey through the pine trees at the foot of a lodge. We knew it was the lake and pulled off the road into a driveway that led to a parking lot. I took the camera out of the un-ceremonial plastic grocery bag and handed the camera to Kurt. Then I opened the lid of the mortuary's black plastic box to fill the grocery bag with some of Seth's ashes to take to the lake. I saw a metal disc atop my son's ashes, the tag that must have gone with his organ-harvested body to the morgue. How like a military dog tag, I thought, and remembered Kurt fearing a draft would involve Seth; I am sure I sighed at his misplaced worries.

I carefully poured some of Seth's ashes into the plastic grocery bag and replaced the metal tag on top of the remaining ashes. For a moment, I felt my fingers next to Seth's little boy fingers sifting ash. I had brought him some from Mt. St. Helens in 1980, when Emily and I were caught during a school trip twenty miles from the mountain's erupting peak. A four-year-old then, Seth spent the day baking a cake with his dad to celebrate the safe return of his sister and her first grade class. Fingering that grey metal, ash-covered tag, I remembered my car, my clothes, everything covered in grey ash, contrasting with the blue, green, red, and yellow candies my son had used to decorate his cake's icing. I could not believe this powder I touched was my son, these ashes lighter than my tears. The day I drove home from that elementary school field trip, I wanted nothing more than to arrive home with my daughter and kiss my worried son. Now I wanted nothing more than to find him merely worried, to kiss him at his wedding.

Kurt and I knew the area of the intended wedding ceremony by the huge stone sculpture Kristen had described, set so its round central opening made a window to the lake. In the intense cold, the three of us spotted steam rising around more sculptures beyond white teepee changing rooms and natural hot springs. Under a frozen grey sky, we walked the desolate winter landscape devoid of vacationers. At the land's point, I knelt and took the bag of ash from my pocket. I thought to spread the ashes at the base of a low bush. It seemed biblical. It just didn't seem right to put the ashes out in the open. I wanted them to remain for at least a little time here where my son would have exchanged vows with Kristen.

Kurt backed away a few feet, camera to his eye. As I put the ashes between bare branches, I worried that the constant wind would blow them back at me, and I would carry them on my clothes instead of leaving them. But the wind died away. And, when I stood up, the sun abruptly burned through the clouds. Now, in the suddenly warm air, I was receiving brilliant sunrays, throbs and throbs of them, directly into my chest.

"Thank you, thank you, thank you," I cried. I thanked Seth for being my son, for all that he brought to my life, for this sun as I returned his ashes to the earth. The clouds around the sun broke farther apart. Jeanne pointed to the shape of an orca.

"It's like the ones he saw each summer at Camp Orkila," I said through tears. "It's like the totem he painted onto his kayak."

Then another orca shape formed in the sky beside the first one, slightly smaller.

"There are two," Jeanne exclaimed.

Seth and Kristen, I thought.

Kurt took a picture of this sky.

Overhead, a pair of ravens soared in the wind. I thought of the spring afternoon when a newly driving Seth had come home to tell us how ravens dive-bombed him as he walked in the neighborhood. They must have been nesting and protecting their young, I told him. Now, though I felt the presence of divinity and received the glorious skies with great thanks, I could not help but think, "If only I could have protected my son." And, even here, I fell silently into my daily what-ifs. What if I'd talked to Seth one more time about the dangers of snowboarding? What if I'd asked him if he was going to wear a helmet? I'd pummeled myself with these questions since the afternoon our family took him off life support, even though I'd had no idea he was going to go snowboarding instead of skiing. What if I'd offered to pay for several massages when he was stressed from moving and starting a new job? Would his body have worked better and kept better control when he was gaining momentum down the slope covered with snowmelt that had iced up suddenly as temperatures dropped? What if I hadn't asked him to call me from his vacation? Maybe something I said left him preoccupied and inattentive to the slopes. What if I'd never divorced his father?

When I'd spoken the litany out loud, Kurt said, "What if you hadn't had a haircut last week?" hoping to let me know that I must not blame myself. But he told me he was running through his own lists of what-ifs: What if he hadn't met us and married me? Seth would have had a different stepfather, one who wouldn't have encouraged him with a drafting table, and he wouldn't have gone into the program he did, and he wouldn't have met Kristen or been snowboarding at Brecken-ridge on December 27, 2000. Here, in death's wake, at the site where Kristen and Seth would have married, we found our-selves bartering away things we most treasured, the way Seth's life intersected with Kristen's, how he brought her to us.

Even in our sorrow and with our tortured thoughts, watch-ing the ravens soar, we felt a miraculous calm at the center of things. It seemed right that we had brought the ashes here. It felt as if Seth could settle into a new existence now that his love with Kristen had in some way been honored here. We shushed the what-if parts of our minds. The sun followed us to the car. I felt Seth saying, *Thanks for coming here. I love you. I am with you.*

Once we had climbed back inside the car, the sunlight van-ished. We drove down the mountain and stopped at a roadside café for something to warm us up. All the waiters looked the way my boy had looked when he attended the University of Colorado. We sat in the café a long time so we could watch those boys in their plaid flannel shirts and ponytails, admire their strong arms and mellow smiles.

We carried the rest of Seth's ashes to our home in Port Townsend to scatter them in Discovery Bay, waters he loved. The day after the funeral service in Seattle, Emily, Jim, and I paddled into the bay in a neighbor's canoe, while Kristen paddled Seth's wooden kayak with the orca painted on its side toward the Olympic Mountains they had hiked together, the mountains where they thought they would teach their children love of the outdoors. Kurt and Ann and Vijay, Jackie and Bob, Seth's half-brothers, and Kristen's sisters and brother-in-law, as well as many uncles and aunts, watched from the shore with flowers in their hands, each blossom sprinkled with some of

Seth's ashes scooped from a hand-painted wooden box that had been a gift one year from Emily's host parents in Japan. Kristen took the box with her in the kayak, and we watched her release some of the ashes into the water. She stopped, though, closed the box, and paddled over to our canoe. She said she couldn't do anymore. It was my turn. She turned and paddled away from the shore, closer to the mountains. I held the small handmade box with whale totems on it upside down over the side of the canoe. Emily, Jim, and I watched the ashes swirl into the water, like a funnel touching down. Kristen took in the Olympics, timeless and large. She seemed to be resolving not to touch down to earth, not until she was ready.

I turned back and saw a necklace of flowers moving from the shoreline toward us. People Seth loved stood at the water's edge, hands empty. I remembered watching Seth from this beach on the day he launched his kayak, smiling broadly as his boat floated, and he paddled away breaking the water's surface not a bit more than necessary. I remembered him paddling once beside me as I paddled in one of the kayaks he'd rented, so a group of us could experience the quiet movement he loved. Now, the necklace of flowers lying smooth on unbroken water mapped the place he'd launched his kayak.

Back inside this house by the bay, this house that Seth designed for us as a high school project when he was seventeen, I studied photographs he had taken of the Grand Canyon, the Brooklyn Bridge, and Times Square. I touched the glass covering the rendering of the house he'd done for his freshman year architecture studio class, and then presented to me on Mother's Day. I took ceramic cups and saucers from the cabinet, a birthday gift from him. How could he have mailed such fragile objects? How could everything be here intact but him?

I looked out the glass back door at the uncovered deck, and I remembered the warm fall when I had stood there after Seth left for his freshman year at college. The builders had not been able to start much before Seth left for Boulder, so I had phoned him often with my questions:

"Why is there a roof over part of the deck, but not over the whole thing where I am standing? Have the builders made a mistake?" I asked him.

"Mom," he answered, either amused that I couldn't remember details of the blueprints or covering up his dismay at how little I applied logic to physical structures, "the uncovered part is your sun deck. The covered one is for rainy days."

Two days after my son's funeral, I stood on the uncovered part of the deck, watching the sun as it rose from behind trees and, later, as it set over Discovery Bay. I did not look away from the rays that teased me into saying hello as if Seth were waving to me across the unusually clear winter sky. These rays drew me from the absence that thudded across my chest like fallen struts.

Now, for the rest of January, I am back in Los Angeles, where I rise at dawn and watch the sun travel up the sky. When the weatherman reminds us that warm air lying over cooler air causes instability and storms, I know that happy memories covering my cold grief will never let me rest.

All day and into the night, I read everything I can about death. I read everything I can about grief. I look at pictures of my son from his childhood to his young adulthood as if I will find physical hints of my inner premonitions. I look at pictures, and he is there in front of me, vibrant and full of love. I have the photo from Gold Mountain and see each day that the scene Kurt captured was just as we remembered it: sun breaking through a slab of grey; orcas curved around the glow. How can I know that Seth is dead and fully believe in his existence? I look each morning at the sun, risen from the dark.

I re-read poems I'd written about him. In 1978, before I entered graduate school in writing, I'd had a memorable afternoon with my then three-year-old son:

Rowing on Lake Union, 1978

On water each crust I feed the birds
falls apart like reason.
The duck's wake resembles ours;
behind us the way grows wider.
My son says he wants to wear his head
on backwards for awhile
to see the last chicken pock fading
between his shoulders, the birthmarks
persistent in their shapes. Secrets
gather in the hollow of his back
like legs budding on a tadpole.
Going forward we celebrate the clouds
billowing after their weight,
the sun's sure fire against the blue.
As we row there is a squeak in the oarlock;
the boat fields our weight on water.
Death unsticks from my dreams now,
leaves with her slippers flapping.

Was death the secret in the hollow of Seth's back? Was that squeak in the oarlock a reminder that life, as we know it, is merely a weight we take on that is as easily dispersed as clouds?

In March, a new issue of *The Sun* magazine arrives. I read an interview with a shaman named Martin Prechtel. "If you are able to feed the other world with your grief, then you can live where your dead are buried," he asserts. Although Seth never lived in Los Angeles, I imagine his ashes traveling from the Northwest waters of Discovery Bay out into the Straits of Juan de Fuca, and then into the Pacific, following me home.

"If this world were a tree," Prechtel says, "then the other world would be the roots—the part of the plant we can't see, but that puts the sap into the tree's veins." I think again of aspens. "The other world feeds this tangible world—the world that can feel pain, that can eat and drink, that can fail; the world that goes around in circles; the world where we die. The other world is what makes this world work. And the way we help the other world continue is by feeding it with our beauty."

Had Seth and I felt the other world together, weightless, out on the water when he was three? I'd written that death had left for the moment. Martin Prechtel's thoughts and metaphorical way of speaking are feeding me. I have been reading about grief every morning, about how I will survive this loss if I can make it meaningful, about how, although the pain won't disappear, I will be able to live with it, that to overcome grief I will have to live in a way that honors my son. I read all this, and it sounds reasonable, but ever since the clouds became orcas, I am not after reason.

A few days later, a friend of mine tells me about a practicing shaman she knows. That the shaman is a friend of my friend is all the reference I require. When I have an interest or a need, help seems to appear. When I lie down on a massage-style table in the shaman's office, I think of my friend's profile as we walked, the tender way she brought up the shaman, and how she had no way of knowing what I had been reading.

The shaman speaks to me softly as she holds my head in her warm hands. "Seth has work to do where he is. He has many guides, Pythagoras among them. He is learning."

I smile, knowing how cool he'd think that was. I think of his dad's words read by the rabbi at the funeral: *As an architect, Seth drew straight lines. He also knew that enough straight lines connected together form a strong circle.* The shaman concentrates and nods her head as if she's gotten news that clarifies a mystery.

"You and Seth have been in earth life together many times. Last time, you were the one to leave first."

I remember my own words in the eulogy: *happiness and sorrow, joy and grief, having and letting go are also one tree.* I'd gotten there with language, and now I'd have to find a way to acknowledge that my being believed the words. The shaman is infusing their meaning into my soul by helping me see myself in a continuing dance with Seth across the millennia.

"Seth is sad," she says, "to see all of you so unhappy, but he wants you to know you were the perfect mother and he loves you."

I think of Seth at sixteen, when he received that perfect score on both the written and the road test for his driver's license. I hear him say those words again: "You know there is no rule you can make now that I can't break. You have to rely on the fact that you did a very good job raising me, and I believe that you did." I lie on the shaman's table, and I cry for my son.

I cry about the summer when Seth was a college sophomore and brought home a young woman he had met at his Seattle summer job. He wanted to court her by making chocolate chip cookies. But I hadn't had kids living at home in awhile and didn't have my pantry stocked with baking supplies. He brought her home to share the treat that he had always been able to make from my stock on hand and nothing was there. "Not a big deal," he said, but to me it remains one—he held the idea that his mother's shelves were always stocked, even when they weren't.

My tears dry a little when I think of how Seth kept his love of cooking and sharing what he'd prepared with others through college and beyond. I think of the graduation party he threw along with his roommates on the lawn in front of the little house they rented. It was a chili feast with Kristen's corn-bread and undergraduates' home-brewed beer.

I call Kristen for the name of Seth's favorite chili cook-book and find a copy to buy. Every day in the late afternoon, I flip through the pages of Norman Kolpas' *The Chili Cookbook*, imagining Seth stirring pots. Some of those afternoons, as I stand at the edge of the dining room table under the new light fixture, flipping through that cookbook, I feel Seth's arm next to mine, his breath blowing my hair. Nights, I long for my bed to shake again. I want to feel that Seth has come to tell me something.

I think frequently of lines the poet Theodore Roethke wrote because he is the poet I was studying all those years ago when Seth and I rowed on Lake Union, and a poet who also lost a son:

> This shaking keeps me steady. I should know.
> What falls away is always. And is near.
> I wake to sleep and take my waking slow.
> I learn by going where I have to go.

Eventually, I begin preparing Seven & Seven and Mexican Mole-Style Turkey Chili from the recipes in the cookbook, allowing myself the feeling of my boy cooking beside me. I do not know a way to feed the other world or how to understand always, though I believed always was with us as the snow fell on our drive to Gold Mountain, as we walked in the cold to Seth's wedding site, as we left his ashes where I know he would have wanted us to, and the sun broke through clouds.

CHAPTER FOUR

VOICE

Camping the Skykomish, 1987

There is white water on this side
of the river; the other side
is clear and placid.
When I turn my back to write
in my notebook at a picnic table
under tall fir, a crow caws.
I see a fisherman, his rowboat
bouncing and knocking
over rocks in the white water.
He is casting for steelhead,
thinking, no doubt, the rough
and rocky side more fruitful.
When the crow takes flight,
his shadow spreads over the wide rocks.
Yesterday, in the woods along
this bank, I found a snail's shell,
whole and unoccupied—
like the voice that will get
me to the other side.

Before Seth died, I was an online editor for a service that coached graduate school applicants in writing compelling personal statements for their applications. Now, when it comes to concentrating on details to persuade admissions committees, I cannot put the elements of other people's life stories together. My boss, who lost a son herself, is more than understanding about not only my need to stop receiving new clients for now, but also my request to pass along clients I had been working with to other editors. A woman in China leaves a message on my phone, so distraught is she by this change of editors. "I am sorry to hear about the loss of your son," she says, "but I don't understand why this means you can't edit my essay."

"How insensitive," everybody says. But, truth be told, I don't think I actually react much differently to her than I do to anyone who expects me to be in any way the same as I was before Seth died.

"Keep your chin up," a favorite aunt who survived cancer tells me when I phone her. She was diagnosed with a malignant tumor when she was pregnant with her son and had to wait till after the birth for treatment. He was born with a tumor on his leg. They both survived, and I admire her, but I don't have it in me to follow her directions.

"I don't want to," I tell her.

"You have Vijay now," my daughter's mother-in-law tells me gently. I hear the depth of her offering, the spinning of trust's strong threads. Certainly, that is true for Emily. But a trade is not what I am imagining.

"I want you to know that Vijay and I are planning to have a baby," Emily says. She thinks the news will help me.

I don't want to be unkind in the face of all this caring, but all I feel is jealousy. My son has not survived. No one can replace him. I cannot give birth to him all over again.

I want to visit Kristen. Being near her and staying in the apartment where Seth had lived is what I want—to breathe the scent of his clothing and drafting table, smile at the way he so neatly stored his papers and books. I think that, as much as we want to be with Kristen since she was closest to Seth, she wants to share time with us because we loved Seth as intensely as she did.

Kurt and I drive to Northern California in early February. When we arrive, we see that Kristen has not changed anything. Seth's worn Birkenstock sandals are by the back door in the kitchen as if he had just come in from emptying the trash. She has rejoined her class at Berkeley's architecture school the second week of the semester. She is in her final year; for now, she wants everything to stay the same.

I walk into Seth's half of the closet, putting my cheeks to his shirtsleeves and admiring the way everything hangs so neatly. My tears wet his favorite deep orange shirt, hanging with the sleeves rolled up, one more wearing in it before the need for laundering. I can see him sitting at his drafting table and preparing dinner at the gigantic old butcher block he and Kristen salvaged from a teardown. I expect him to play his new favorite CD on the stereo and to tease me about bringing too much food with us.

Kristen and I don't eat that many sweets.

We have lots of garlic. You didn't need to bring a whole braid from Gilroy, but we'll use it.

Come and walk to the park. We can toss a Frisbee around while Kristen finishes at the studio.

I wonder what Kristen will do now with four bikes—the two of his and the two of hers they kept inside in the front hallway. I keep seeing my young man in his biking shorts, his curly hair pressed down from wearing a helmet and his electric blue eyes bright from an invigorating ride. I imagine him trying to figure out a better place to keep those bikes handy, but safe.

They tried their best with this apartment, I think, but it could not muster the charm of the little bungalow they lived in until their landlady decided to have her own son move in there. At the bungalow, they'd eaten beside a stained glass window. They'd walked through a lovely arched and oak-trimmed doorway from the kitchen.

I can see Seth talking with his landlady, who lived around the same bungalow-lined courtyard. I am sure that Seth was feeling more like a neighbor than a tenant when he stood beside the roses the landlady tended and told her that Kristen was applying to graduate architecture schools for the following fall, and they hoped she'd be accepted at UC Berkeley, only blocks from where they were living; however, as back-up she had to apply to other schools. I know it came as quite a shock to Seth when the landlady decided what he said meant they were going to be leaving, and she told her son, who was quite comfortable where he was, that she had a vacancy coming up and wanted him to move in. Seth was a skilled and conscientious tenant, keeping things tasteful and in good repair, not only for his landlady, but for others who rented or owned around the common courtyard. I imagine that the landlady felt gratitude toward Seth. I imagine just the possibility he might leave thrust her into considering that she might never get a better tenant. Thus, perhaps, it was time, I imagine she thought, to bring her son closer.

Seth said if the landlady had just told them she wanted her son to move in, he would have gladly looked for a different place, but being misrepresented angered him. The place he and Kristen found in a hurry wasn't really to Seth's liking, and

Kristen offered to move again if the apartment made Seth too unhappy. But it was only for eight or nine months, he reasoned. I sat on Kristen's couch, and I caught myself thinking "what if" again. What if they hadn't taken this apartment? What if the landlady hadn't felt the sudden need to tell her son to move into the bungalow? What if Kristen hadn't disliked an apartment in a lovelier location but with a strange layout? What if, what if, what if…

In moments like this one, it becomes hard to remind myself that things don't go smoothly for anyone all the time, but people don't usually die of it. I think of significant disappointments in all of our lives. Emily hadn't made the list for being the exchange student she wanted to be the first time she tried. I had been only runner-up for a full-time tenure track position I wanted, one I believed I needed to support myself after my divorce. Kurt had moved his company once to merge with another company, and it didn't work out. I knew crushing disappointment. I knew how we usually lived through it. I know I will someday have to let go of this what-if string of questions. The events that circle in my mind were not the cause of Seth's death. They linger with me because they tell me more about who my son was. And the more I think about who he was, the sweeter his life becomes, and the more miserable I become thinking of anyone or anything that most recently impinged on his good nature.

After we return home, I am restless through the night. I live for sunrise and my ritual of greeting the Los Angeles sun from the stairwell window that faces east, of remembering the moment when the sun broke through the clouds at Gold Mountain and Jeanne pointed out the orcas that had formed in the sky.

After the ball of fire is too bright to look at directly, and Kurt is dressing for work, I go to my desk to read the emails that continue coming with memories of Seth. I answer friends of my son's and thank them for sending us their stories and digital photos. I answer my daughter's emails about books that matter to her for healing. Always, it is the ones with stories in them rather than advice. My daughter recommends a collection of essays called *In Lieu of Flowers* by Nancy Cobb, a woman who retraces her mother's young adult life in New York. I am reading Richard Elder's *Into the Valley and Out Again*. Reading others' stories of loss, such as Melody Beattie's about her young teen son's death while skiing, is like reading an extension of the emails and letters about Seth. Each one of the sons is Seth. Each had a life that seemed to intensify just before he died. Their mothers all noticed something changing.

I continue exchanging email with Seth's dad, who is sharing memories from our marriage as well as more stories from those gathered around him in Seattle. One of those is about a colleague of his, who was taken by the closing words in my eulogy with Kurt:

> When you sit on a bench and watch people or the sunset, think of a young man who wanted to make sure there were more places in this world to sit quietly and soak things in, more places for human connections and for caring about one another and the habitats we live in.

J. Michael Rona wants to fund a bench in Seth's honor, he has told Jim, and Jim has decided that putting it outside the doors of the Port Townsend Marine Science Center is a good idea. Seth had enjoyed exploring the idea of designing "in place" and did his graduate thesis work based on a redesign for the Port Townsend Marine Science Center. The Science Center is situated on land that was an Indian gathering place, and then an early United States fort, as well as a World War II military installation before becoming a campground and center for the study of the arts and the environment. Seth was convinced that good design honored the history of all previous uses for a parcel of land, and for his thesis, without the budget or committee input that real world projects have, Seth designed a new Center that took into account the land's history.

Jim has already gone to work with the Center to create a bench. He wanted to include Kristen's name on the plaque. The director of the Center wanted us to change sunset to sunrise since their site faced east. The words became:

In memory of Seth Bender (1975-2000)
and the love he shared with Kristen Belt

As you sit on a bench and watch people or the sunrise, think of a young couple who wanted to make sure there were more places in this world to sit quietly and soak things in, more places for human connections and for caring about one another and the habitats we live in.

Jim said Seth had long been an anchor to his large family and friends. He had written program notes for the funeral service that included Seth's words when he instructed his young half brothers in flying kites, "Pull down with both hands, and it will jump into the sky. A little movement with your wrists is all it takes. The faster it dives, the faster it will climb." Whatever Seth was doing, Jim wrote, whether a design project, planning a cooking adventure, or settling into a living space, the lessons were the same: work with Seth, and you would see how to create beauty and order.

How had Seth become this kind of person? I search my memory for clues, and all I find are moments that break my heart.

"I want to see my dad!" four-year-old Seth sometimes cried hard before bedtime at my little rental house after our separation.

"You will see your dad, Sweetie. Tomorrow he is picking you up from daycare."

"No, I want to see him now. I want to see you both at the same time."

Now, together, at the same time, we are telling stories about our fine young man.

Mornings after reading email, I get up from my desk and roam around my Los Angeles condo, thinking of Seth's visit for a weekend when Kurt and I were first putting things together after we moved in. I stand by the television cabinet Seth had climbed atop to fasten a heavy piece of wooden folk art onto the wall. I smooth my hands over the butcher block he showed Kurt how to sand with the electric sander we bought him as a thank you present for coming to help us. I smell the mineral oil on it that he told me to start using on a regular basis. I stare at the pot rack he fastened, with Kurt's help, to the kitchen ceiling, and I see his fingerprints on the chrome. I go to the faucet and examine the caulking Seth used to seal the gap between the kitchen sink and the tiled kitchen counter.

"See how it's getting better toward the back, here, where I was able to get the applicator to give me a thinner line? I wish I had started from the back," I remember him saying.

"It's all beautiful to me," I had told him, but that was Seth. As his father had written, "The job always had to be done right and done well. Once, as a five-year-old, he had to ask his grandmother where he could find some elbow grease, so he could do a better job of cleaning the kitchen."

Weeks go by as I keep reading and collecting stories and pictures from the people Kurt said were adding themselves to "Team Seth." I try writing my own words, but few come right now. I decide to invent an assignment for myself from a poem by Robert Desnos that I had enjoyed teaching: "The Voice of Robert Desnos," translated from the French by William Kulik. A particular excerpt continues to move me:

> I call tornadoes and hurricanes
> storms typhoons cyclones
> tidal waves
> earthquakes
> I call the smoke of volcanoes and the smoke of cigarettes
> the rings of smoke from expensive cigars
> I call lovers and loved ones
> I call the living and the dead
> I call gravediggers I call assassins
> I call hangmen pilots bricklayers architects
> assassins
> I call the flesh
> I call the one I love
> I call the one I love
> I call the one I love
> the jubilant midnight unfolds its satin wings
>   and perches on my bed
> the belfries and the poplars bend to my wish

the former collapse the latter bow down
those lost in the fields are found in finding me
the old skeletons are revived by my voice
the young oaks cut down are covered with foliage
the scraps of cloth rotting on the ground and in the earth
    snap to at the sound of my voice like a flag of rebellion

In his book, *How to Read a Poem and Fall in Love with Poetry*, which I used as a text with my students, Edward Hirsch writes that, in this poem, Desnos exemplifies what the Russian poet, Marina Tsvetaeva, said about poets: "A poet is carried far away by speech, the way of comets / is the poet's way." Hirsch says that "entirely carried away by speech toward a beloved other," Desnos is "taking the comet's path away from the daylight and into the night mind," and "giving full-throated voice to the immensity of desire."

Ever since I arrived back in Los Angeles from the Society of Southwest Authors writer's conference I taught at, people do not seem to be hearing my voice. The few times I do go out with friends or speak to someone behind a counter, people say, "What? Can you repeat that?" Whether I am responding to a well meant condolence, trying to converse with a friend on a walk, or ordering a half pound of sliced provolone, I am somehow not speaking loud enough for anyone to hear me. It seems as if I do not want to make myself heard. Writing, I can at least borrow from Desnos' syntax and strategy. Maybe it will work and free words where tears dwelt. To find out what the voice of Sheila Bender sounds like behind the hidden sobs, I write a title on a blank piece of paper: "The Voice of Sheila Bender." Immediately, I know what I want to call to. After mornings of tackling the drafting and redrafting, I have this poem:

The Voice of Sheila Bender
After Robert Desnos

I call to the ski slopes of Breckenridge;
I call to the trees on the slopes of Breckenridge;
I call to the snow and the ice hanging in their branches;
I call to the snow on the run and the melted layer iced
   over;
I call to my son, to my son in his thermal clothing, to my
   son
twenty-five years old and snowboarding, headed into the
   trees.
I call to him to tumble off the board, not to worry
about looking clumsy, not to worry about finishing the
   run.
I call and I call, but he does not hear me.
I call over the weeks between then and now
to the hospital and time of death: 3:30 December 28th
   2000
but my son does not tumble where I want him to.
I call clear as the moon, single eye I howl beneath.
I call and I call. She weeps holy water over my eyelids,
hands, knees, feet that must carry me the rest of my days.
In the snow, I see sadness crystallize, hear my voice
force the follicles in my body to burst along their single
   seams,
spread seeds, the seeds I see in sunlight and my son
everywhere, everywhere I call.

When a poet friend asks if I will contribute a poem to
her website dedicated to helping people through difficult life

circumstances and passages, I re-title the poem, "I Call to the Ski Slopes of Breckenridge" and send it to her.

Most importantly, copying Robert Desnos' strategy helped me find sound that matched the intensity and enormity of my sadness, something that daily life didn't allow.

Now people less and less frequently ask me to repeat what I have just said.

CHAPTER FIVE

BREAKTHROUGH

If We, 1985

If we are a body,
it is of trees,
from their tall trunks
the sound of doors opening.
If we are a tree,
the leaves are lobed
and feathery gathering light.
If we are light,
clouds are moving fast
across the moon.
If we are moon,
we are the new one
rejuvenating.
If we rejuvenate
we are the world,
each of us a continent
and each a bridge.

In early spring, we make another trip to Berkeley to attend a memorial Seth's friends have organized in a redwood grove where he often biked. It is chilly the day of the memorial, and young couples who worked with Seth remodeling their homes bring very welcome coffee and bagels for us all. After a brief ceremony in which these vibrant young people present Kristen with a handmade box filled with pictures of Seth and her, we sit in a circle in the woods, recalling Seth. This is his most recent life. We hear stories about his work with others and about hikes and sailing. His high school girlfriend, who now lives in Modesto and often still spoke with Seth, talks about how she will continue to talk with him, so well does she know the way he would counsel her about choices and plans.

Wondering what I might add to the stories, I remember a call Seth made to me once during architecture school when Kristen was in Denmark on a study abroad course.

"Hi, Mom." Seth's voice was happy.

"What's up, kiddo?" I asked, bringing myself up from the deep concentration I fall into when I am writing.

"I just came back from having coffee across from the architecture building. I was frustrated in my designing, but now I've had a breakthrough."

"What's the breakthrough?"

"Well, we have to design a low income housing project that will motivate pride of ownership, and I just couldn't get anywhere in designing so that I could create a neighborhood where people feel connected and will care for their homes. But then I started sketching your house in Seattle, and I was able to make a good design."

"That's what writers call starting with what you know," I told him. I wasn't insulted that he found the house I bought after divorcing his father something he could use to design for low-income people. I had loved the house, built in 1913, with its handmade stairway and simple floor plan. I had always called it my "housey house." I felt comfortable the moment I walked in and so did everyone else who came there. It was the house where Seth had kept his trains in the basement and made videos in the living room and cracked the ceiling plaster below his room with the bass on his stereo turned up high.

I loved that my son was drawing on the elements of that house to produce something others, no matter their lack of money, would enjoy living in. I was glad he thought to draw my "housey house" and go from there with his ideas.

I tell this story of Seth's breakthrough at the gathering in the redwood trees. Afterward, Richard, a social worker in his forties, who lived next door to the bungalow Kristen and Seth were forced to leave, tells us about Seth at Halloween. He'd hidden behind a citrus tree to scare the trick-or-treaters who came up the sidewalk with a big "Boo." I can hear him saying, "That's part of what Halloween is about, right?" I smile, thinking about my son as part of his neighborhood and a part of the silliness of that night.

At Seth's funeral in Seattle, I'd told Richard that, when I'd said goodbye to Seth at Thanksgiving, I'd heard a voice inside me saying, "I hope he'll hug you goodbye. It may be the last time he will be able to." I also told him about my last conversation with Seth, when Seth was in Kansas City on Christmas Eve day. I had called in the early afternoon and spoken with Jackie, who told me Seth was out with Kristen and Bob. She'd added, like those who feel they have someone else's charge, that she'd have him return my call.

Seth called me back, and I said, "Jackie told me you and Kristen decided on china to register for today and that you were the one to notice it."

"Yeah, I never thought I'd have anything like that in my life, but it is pretty." Jackie knew that many of the people coming to the wedding from Kansas City wanted to buy the kids something more traditional than the tools they said they were going to register for. Buying table settings was more a Kansas City thing than a Berkeley thing. I hoped they'd register for the tools, as well. It pleased me to think of them making furniture and remodeling the fixer home they planned on buying when Kristen finished school and they were both working for architecture firms. To my mind, beautiful fine china goes well with fine woodworking.

Fatigue seemed to cloak Seth's voice as we talked a bit more. I didn't think the fatigue was from figuring out what to register for. Seth enjoyed design and using simple materials to promote a high quality of life. I didn't think it was the time difference or the rush from work to his night flight the day before. He acclimated well when he traveled.

"You sound tired," I said.

"Yeah, it's been busy," he said, and I remembered that Jackie said she didn't really want to leave to go skiing the next day because it felt like an interruption of the wedding planning.

"Well, I'll call you after Christmas at the ski village condo," I said brightly. But in his okay, I heard a catch in his voice, a wavering, as if he didn't know if that would be possible. Maybe he worried that he couldn't commit to being near the phone.

"Jackie gave me the number when I spoke with her this afternoon," I offered, not wanting Seth's hesitation to hang in the air. "I'll speak to you in a few days," I said. "I love you."

But as I hung up, the hesitation still rang in my ears. Jackie wanted me to have the number in case I needed to talk to Seth because of my father's illness. But I knew I wanted it so

I could check in on Seth. He was a competent young man on a vacation with a competent and lovely family, but I felt something ominous. The sound of his hesitation ultimately became one more affirmation that something in him knew his life was ending.

At the funeral in Seattle, Richard had tried to comfort me, saying Seth was just tired after making so many decisions concerning his future—he had decided to leave a job he liked as assistant architect on a construction site and take a lower paying design studio job important to getting his architect's license. He had proposed to Kristen. And they were forced to move. He needed the rest all young men need at times, this neighbor said, drawing on his training and experience.

But this thinking didn't change my feeling that I had had a premonition. I told Richard the voice in my head on Thanksgiving was hooked into fear I'd carried these three years of Seth's winter vacations. The last time I'd seen Seth breathing on his own, this unbidden voice was telling the truth.

I couldn't shake the feeling that something in Seth knew he would die soon, too. On Thanksgiving Day, Seth, Kristen, Emily, and Vijay had driven from Northern California to our house in Los Angeles. It was Seth's idea for all of them to leave the Bay Area very early in order to arrive in Los Angeles in time to help us cook the Thanksgiving meal. He was going to call and give us an update on the progress they were making, so we could better plan the cooking. When the phone rang at 10 AM, Kurt and I knew it was the kids.

"How are you doing?" I asked, expecting a traffic update.

"Not very well," Seth said, and I thought of the expression, "bumper-to-bumper." Not very well, he continued, because he had fainted after they stopped for breakfast and required

stitches on a forehead wound. I knew the call was orchestrat-
ed—that the kids had waited for him to feel well enough to
place the call, so I would not worry as much as if someone else's
voice informed me. He was disappointed to be holding up the
journey. He felt okay physically, and the cut wasn't too bad. He
had probably just had a vagal situation—being warm, having
a full stomach, then getting up quickly, and then not having
enough blood reach his brain. This had happened to him a few
times in his childhood. But something else was brewing this
time. I heard it in his, "Not very well."

Kurt and I resumed our cooking, unsettled and knowing
we'd complete it without the kids' help. Though neither of us
said anything to the other about it, it turned out we both feared
more bad news.

The kids arrived at three, and a quiet Seth couldn't not
help put finishing garnishes on the meal. But, when we ate
Thanksgiving dinner around four, Seth was not himself, not as
enthusiastic as he would otherwise have been over the squash
and apple soup, the sausage stuffing. He didn't take the hearty
second and even third helpings we started expecting when he
turned fourteen. He was certainly shaken by the fainting, but
there was something else afoot, too.

All weekend, when he rose from sitting, he got up slowly,
trying to avoid a trigger to fainting. When the kids left for
home, we did hug goodbye, and the length of the hug Seth
gave me pleased me. I tried to discount the thought that this
might be the last time I'd see Seth. I tried to chide myself for
the feeling and ignore the musty smell of it, like something
stuffed far back in a drawer.

I was worried about whether Seth would be feeling up to
snuff by the time of his trip to Kansas City and Colorado.

Later, I remembered how, when Jackie told me in our phone conversation the day before Christmas that she wished they didn't have to leave Kansas City, she also told me she felt she couldn't disappoint Barbara and Sonny, who had signed up for snowboarding lessons. The words, "That's a dangerous sport," popped to my lips, but I didn't say them. I stuffed my feeling about Seth's being in danger away again with a falsely soothing thought like, "Well, I don't have to worry about Seth snowboarding. Since he isn't taking lessons, he won't be snowboarding. He'll be skiing." He said he was feeling fine and hadn't felt faint at all lately, just tired from all the registering, I reassured myself. The medics told him the fainting was probably nothing more than blood not getting to his head fast enough when he stood up after sitting in a warm place for awhile. I knew he hadn't yet been able to get in to see the right specialist at his HMO. I tried my best to be rational and go with his reports of feeling fine.

Now, I realize Jackie had said "Barbara and Sonny" out of habit—the names of her daughter and son-in-law just sliding off her tongue together. She had meant Seth and Sonny. The two young men were going to do the snowboarding.

At the funeral, I had told Richard that I couldn't really say anything to Seth over the phone about my fears. I didn't want to frighten him, and how do you say, "I just can't stop feeling scared," when nothing is amiss? Moreover, now that he was to be married, I could be very annoying if I treated him anything like my child, so I held back on my motherly concern and held on to what the doctor had said. But my feeling was that the faint on the way to Los Angeles on Thanksgiving was not only about getting up too fast when he was warm and full. It was a warning.

Seeing Richard by the coffee at the memorial service, I am thinking about how, since Seth's death, I've read somewhere that all of us choose our lives and the major events in them before we are born and that we give ourselves three possible exit times. I can think of two near misses for Seth during his childhood and late adolescence. When he was seven and just home from a trip to St. Thomas with his dad's family, he looked the wrong way for oncoming traffic. He was holding my hand, but decided to jump out to start crossing. I watched a car approaching fast and Seth jumping around as if motion alone would keep him safe. Somehow, the car missed Seth. At eighteen, he had a few years of sleepwalking history. One night at a friend's house, he got up from sleep and fell down concrete steps. For awhile, nobody found him unconscious and bleeding with broken teeth and a broken nose. Now, these seem like dress rehearsals, almost, times he or some other power decided he must stay.

Jim spoke with the organ donor coordinator, who reported that the examination of Seth's heart showed it was normal, injured by the stress of the accident and not structurally abnormal, which would have been a possible cause of fainting. The head of the ski patrol, Jim said, shared the reports of a young man who was at the scene and a person on a nearby lift. They saw Seth going fast downhill and trying to break his speed; they saw him catch the front edge of the board and fall forward into the trees. "So, a dumb accident after all," Jim wrote. He, too, had worried that Seth had had a physical problem contributing to his accident.

I refill my cup of coffee, thinking how those watching Seth snowboard airborne into a tree must have felt like I did, watching that car a hair's breadth away, knowing Seth knew the problem, was doing what he could to escape. And there was Kristen, waiting for some time without knowing about the accident, my son once again injured and his friends at first unaware.

In the chilly redwood grove, Seth's former landlady walks up beside me to refill her coffee cup. I smile weakly. The memory she shared as we sat in the redwood grove concerned Seth's dislike of the ants that had invaded his kitchen. He had asked her to please keep her outdoor garbage cans somewhere other than adjacent to his kitchen, believing this would cut down on the invasion of ants. How silly that was, she said, how much he just didn't understand California and its ants. I find it grating to listen to her talk about Seth's fallibilities, if his perception about keeping ants out of his house could even have been called that. Seth maintained strong habits when it came to security and cleanliness. Instead of laughing lightly as I think she meant for us to do, I began to think she'd moved her son into the bungalow Seth loved because she didn't want to move her garbage cans. I don't like this anger in myself. People have been commenting for months on my seeming lack of anger over Seth's death. Well, here it is, landing on his landlady. What if this woman hadn't made Seth move?

To divert my thoughts, I go to thank another woman for her story about Seth. She told of asking Seth and Kristen to design an addition to her home. Seth had patiently explained changes to her ideas that would help optimize the natural light in her new space. She spoke eloquently about how much that light now meant to her each day as she worked in that addition.

As I stand sipping coffee, Richard approaches me. He wants to tell me about a dream he had in the time since we

spoke at the funeral. In it, Seth told him, "My mom is right."
This sounds so much like my son. He always talked succinctly
about important things. He was correcting Richard's social-
worker explanation. I am grateful. It seems again that dreams,
not reason, are the friends of those who grieve.

Home again in Los Angeles after the weekend in Berkeley,
I resume my morning ritual of watching the sunrise and read-
ing about grief. I resume going to my desk. To help myself
write, I look in a book I'd written, *Writing Personal Poetry*, to
find out how I had encouraged others:

> We write poetry for the same reasons our eyes
> watch finches eat seed from a sunflower or our ears lis-
> ten to the lacy hem of a lake's edge sweeping across a
> pebbled shore. We write for the same reasons we watch
> automobiles on rainy days move into traffic like ants on
> spilled lemonade. We are lulled by the world and joined
> to it by our very cells. We search for those junctures we
> know are there. Writing poems is a way to search for
> and experience the joining.

But I am not sure if I can write well enough to join with the
other world, the one I am interested in now.

Emily and Kristen are still attending a grief support group.
Emily tells me of the account they heard from a mother about
seeing her dead son appear in her house. I have read stories
about those who've lost people seeing them in their rooms at
night. My cousin, whose husband died suddenly, told me she
and her daughter had both seen him the same night in the hall-
ways of their home. Emily and I long to see Seth, but we have
the same thought: we don't want him to scare us.

Finally, Seth comes to *me* in a dream. He is wearing his deep orange shirt, the sleeves rolled up as usual. He is happy, sitting on a bench beside me in a garden. It matters very much to me that he looks well, bursting with health. It matters that he brings serenity to me. It matters that this feeling lasts well past the dream.

Can I write the experience the dream gave me? Jackie, Bob, and Kristen have invited Kurt and me to Kansas City to join them over the June weekend that we would have had the wedding. I want to know what a poem might say to comfort us.

I give myself another assignment. It is from another poem I taught, Elizabeth Bishop's "One Art":

One Art

The art of losing isn't hard to master;
so many things seem filled with the intent
to be lost that their loss is no disaster.

Lose something every day. Accept the fluster
of lost door keys, the hour badly spent.
The art of losing isn't hard to master.

Then practice losing farther, losing faster:
places, and names, and where it was you meant
to travel. None of these will bring disaster.

I lost my mother's watch. And look! my last, or
next-to-last, of three loved houses went.
The art of losing isn't hard to master.

I lost two cities, lovely ones. And, vaster,
some realms I owned, two rivers, a continent.
I miss them, but it wasn't a disaster.

—Even losing you (the joking voice, a gesture
I love) I shan't have lied. It's evident
the art of losing's not too hard to master
though it may look like (*Write* it!) like disaster.

I reread Edward Hirsch's assertion that Elizabeth Bishop's poem is "a kind of instruction manual on loss." To him, "One Art" exemplifies the kind of poem in which "form structures experience." In this case, the form is a villanelle; nineteen lines

are divided into six stanzas—five tercets and one quatrain—
that turn on two rhymes and two refrains. The middle lines of
each stanza rhyme, as do the first and third lines throughout
the poem. The first and third lines of each stanza become the
refrain of alternate stanzas and the final two lines of the poem.
What strikes me in Hirsch's words about the form is his state-
ment that the circularity of the repetitions is blown open by
the forward movement of other lines. And then I notice he
wrote that the poem is an example of the author's "long ap-
prenticeship to poetry and even longer apprenticeship to the
art of loss."

Though I have a longer apprenticeship to poetry than to
the art of loss, I feel that the villanelle form might offer a way
for me to work out my thoughts. I also feel that the villanelle
with its required repetitions is the right form for me to work in
since I don't think anyone grieving the loss of a child progresses
so much as circles and circles around pain. In the months since
Seth's death, my editing boss has told me how much she resents
the idea of having to "gain resolution" concerning the death of
her son. She doesn't want a resolution, which is an ending. She
would miss him too much.

With a copy of "One Art" open on my left, I sit at my desk
for hours. Eventually, I have a poem:

A New Theology
For Seth Bender, 1975-2000

Who has no likeness of a body and has no body
is my son, now five months dead
but in my dreams, my dreams he brings the peace in
    gardens.

And I see him in his smile and he is hardy
in the rolled up sleeves of his new shirt, well-fed
when he has no likeness of a body and has no body.

I see him next to me in conversation at a party
and I believe that he is fine because this is what he said,
because in my dreams, my dreams I sit with him in
    gardens.

The nights he comes, the cats moan long and sorry.
I believe they see his spirit entering my head,
he who has no likeness of a body and has no body.

In my life, accepting death comes slowly,
but the midwifery of sadness and of shock bleeds
afterbirth, dreams that bring the peace in gardens.

I know that he is far and he is here and he is holy.
Under sun, I feel the energy it takes to come away from
    God
who has no likeness of a body and has no body
who is in my dreams, the dreams that bring me gardens.

I show the poem to Kurt and he sits down immediately to format a copy on the computer that will complement the 5x8-inch prints we had made of Seth's sky at Gold Lake. We go to Kinko's to make copies of the poem for everyone who would have been in the wedding party. Then we purchase plain Lucite frames and place the two pieces of art together.

By writing this poem, I have found a way to transcend daily life, a way to go beyond connection with the world as I knew it and begin to feel a part of the world my son now inhabits. Can I continue to do this? Can I learn to feed that world with impressions from this one, as Prechtel said we must?

CHAPTER SIX

PORT OF CALL

The Small Gestures I Remember Him By

Each night when my father returned from work,
he climbed the steps of our split-level house
headed for his bedroom where he emptied
the chewing gum and coins from his suit pants'
pockets onto the top of his highboy dresser,
white handkerchief, neatly folded, too.
I heard the sound of the metal on wood
between words of their conversation, my mother
and father behind the closed door of their bedroom.
It was good the way they reunited, the way he came
downstairs in chinos and a tee shirt, his lightly
starched white shirt saved to wear one more day,
his pants and suit coat neatly hung on the valet
my mother bought for this purpose.
Then to the kitchen, where he spread a dish towel
horizontally across the front of his pants
and tucked the top of it into his belt.
I can still see the suntan on his left arm,
the one that during his long commute
rested on the rolled down window of his mustard
colored Chevy. And then the chopping as he
helped with dinner, the onions, the tomatoes,
the way he always asked, "What else?"

In mid-April, when the mountain passes along Interstate 5 in California and Oregon are finally clear of ice and snow, I pick out new tires for a Toyota Tercel I have bought from friends, and I drive to Seattle. My plan is to leave a car at my parents' house so, when I come to the Northwest to write, I will no longer have to rent or borrow a car. I want to spend more and more time in the house Seth designed, in the landscape he had planned to return to after Kristen graduated, near the kayak he'd built, the beach he launched it from, and the hammock he brought for us to relax in. I am soothed by the sense of balance he put in those rooms, a sense he seems to have been born with, that brings contemplation and activity together into time meaningfully spent.

Most of all, this visit, I want to see my father. My mother told me he could no longer remain upright, even in a chair. He leans badly to the left, she says, and sitting, grows tired very quickly. Weak as he's become, though, he isn't talking about endings.

"We've already made our wishes known about not being revived in a medical emergency," my mother says bravely. But that document doesn't cover the decision she is facing now about communicating to my father, who isn't talking about his death, that *she* is preparing for the end.

My mother's angst absorbs me. She and my father have been married since they were eighteen. She is doing what they agreed they would do for one another, whoever needed it first: provide a home, even through terminal illness. She has had doorways enlarged to accommodate his wheelchair and bought matching hospital beds so he can lie comfortably and adjust the bed for help getting out of it, and so she can sleep next to him, as she has for fifty-seven years. She's hired aides for during the daytime, but keeps their evenings just for them. When it became difficult to help him in the bathroom and in and out of bed, she hired additional aides until his bedtime, and then to arrive first thing in the morning. Only a year ago, my dad was staying up later than she was to watch the eleven o'clock news, as he always had. When I visited and sat with him, I thought of when I was in college, and he called after the late news, Eastern Standard time. My time zone was two hours behind his, and he wanted to check out the student unrest he'd witnessed on the air.

"What is going on there?" he asked. I looked out my window and gave him first-hand accounts. While he'd seen video of students throwing rocks, I was seeing police with billy clubs breaking the first-floor windows of old homes divided into college apartments and dragging students to the street.

Eleven years later, he asked another version of this question when I told my parents Jim and I were separating. They loved Jim, whom they had known since I met him at sixteen. They were afraid for Emily and Seth, then six and four. They didn't think I knew what I was doing.

"What is going on?" my father asked in phone calls, as I struggled to re-establish my life.

I couldn't explain that I'd married a young man he and my mother approved of, whom I met when I was young, because that was how I could leave home with their blessings. I couldn't explain how the marriage had turned out to be a way to delay exploring who I was. I couldn't explain that having children made me realize that, to raise them to be who they were, I had to be willing to be who I was.

I assured him that Jim and I had worked out a solid joint custody situation. He wanted to know what I would do to support myself.

"I'm going to graduate school to be a poet, Dad. I'm going to write poems."

"But what are you going to do?" he asked again.

"I'm going to write poems," I said again.

"What are you going to do?" he repeated, as if I hadn't given him an answer.

"I'm a teacher, Dad. I'll also keep teaching." I felt him relax, 3,000 miles from where I held the phone.

But even when I didn't explain myself, he never stopped being there for me. When my parents came to visit after I'd moved into a 1913 house with no closets on the first floor, my father took me shopping for a hall stand, saying I needed a place to hang my hat. For years, I hung a grey felt fedora I took to wearing on the hook above my children's quilted winter parkas—red for Seth, powder blue for Emily.

Now, three days after I loaded the powder blue Tercel with my laptop, luggage, and books, I pull into my parents' Seattle-area driveway in mid-afternoon sunlight.

My dad sits propped upright in a wheelchair stuffed with pillows. He has a feeding tube now and has lost more weight. The past year, even with his swallowing failing him, he still loved to eat. But he couldn't get enough nutrition down, and we worried. He told us not to, saying he was merely back to his Navy weight.

As soon as I kiss him hello, his new aide begins wheeling him toward the door to see the car he's worried for days about me driving. With a quick wave to my mother, I follow.

"How much did you pay for it?" my father asks in the softest voice I'd ever heard him use. Parkinson's disease has drastically reduced the strength of his vocal cords.

"Twelve hundred dollars," I tell him, wishing he were standing next to me and kicking the tires.

"Let's go for a ride," he says.

I am not surprised at his request to find out for himself how the car runs, and it makes me happy to show him what a buy I've gotten. The son of Eastern European immigrants who worked hard to achieve their American dream, he usually wants everything he owns to be new—houses, furniture, cars. But when I received a summer internship that required driving to the Goethels Bridge tolls collection unit office in Elizabeth, New Jersey, he proudly bought me a used car—and he loved the black and white Rambler I headed out in every morning as much as I did. As I economized in making my first homes and bought used furniture like he had been raised with, he shared his memories of growing up with immigrants and first-generation Americans, of boiled chickens every Friday night, of wearing knickers and not being allowed to have the long pants he longed for until he was fourteen, of having to call his siblings Brother and Sister, rather than by their names. Once, when he and my mother still lived in the suburbs of New York City and I came East to visit friends on the city's lower East Side, he picked me up at the cramped, walk-up apartment like ones he'd left behind as a youth. I saw uncharacteristic fondness in his eyes as we walked to where he'd parked. He seemed happy to be back where so many of his relatives had first lived upon entering the country.

While my mother puts together a late lunch, my dad's aide slides him into the front passenger seat of the Tercel and takes a seat behind him, where she can extend her arm to keep him upright as I drive. Through the passenger side door, I snap his seat belt into place and walk around the car to take my seat behind the wheel. As we drive the blocks near his house, I get up enough speed to shift from first to second and third at least once. My dad isn't saying much, and I imagine he is remembering the first cars he'd driven, especially the old standard transmission Pontiac he'd bought when I was just born and he was finishing four years of college in two on the GI bill. I'd been surprised to learn that my strait-laced dad had routinely played poker at the veterans' Diesel Housing Unit for gas money, so he could commute ten miles to the University of Richmond, where he was not only a student, but also a teaching assistant.

Less than five minutes after we get in the Tercel, my dad is fatigued and asks that we pull back into his driveway. His aide helps him into the wheelchair. He puts his right hand to the back of his head, as if smoothing his short-clipped hair. "It's a good car," he tells me. I follow as the aide wheels him inside and helps him back to bed.

I am worried that my dad will not be alive on Seth's wedding date, when I plan to give everyone the picture Kurt took at Gold Lake, but I long to talk with my parents about what happened. I've brought a framed 8x10-inch print of the picture to present to them now.

"How peaceful," my mother says, when I show it to her, even before I tell her where it was taken. When I do, she tells me to take the picture into the bedroom for my dad to see right now. As he holds it, I sit by his bedside, telling him the story of the sky that day. Without comment on the story or how much we all miss Seth or how sad he is for me, he points to where he wants the picture, a spot directly in his view as he lies on his bed, unable to turn by himself. He can't talk much more even if he wanted to, but I realize I don't need words now. I remember my cousins telling me that, at Seth's funeral, my dad whispered, "It should have been me." Clearly, he wishes he could have given his life not to lose Seth and doesn't need to talk about loss. But, without talk, I don't know how to acknowledge this. His response about where to put the picture contains all the words I need.

Several days later, I take a short break to visit Port Townsend and write. It is still difficult to concentrate. I eat chilled Alaska King Crab and barbequed mussels with a friend from England. The taste of seafood always transports her back to her childhood and to memories of her parents and sisters and brothers, she says. Her family was poor and had little to eat most days during the war, but, when they could, they visited her grandmother in a seaside town and ate well from their catch. So, when she eats seafood, she doesn't talk. She lets the taste bring everyone back to her. I will try that, I think—assign tomatoes and onions and cucumbers to bring back memories of my dad, who always prepared salad before he barbequed steak, who chopped ingredients for Sunday morning omelets. Pistachio ice cream and Halvah will work, too.

I see myself chopping the onions for chili and thinking of my father and of Seth, who, by dying first, has somehow become my father and my father's father. When I think this way, I hear echoes of a refrain from Jewish prayers, "My God and God of my fathers." The philosopher Martin Buber wrote that the repetition expresses the idea that, though many have worshiped before us, each of us creates our own belief in God ourselves, out of our particular perceptions and experiences. Fathers, both gods and human beings, inspire and disappoint, empower us and take that power away. Sometimes, we leave our fathers and become prodigal. Sometimes, we return with something humble in our hearts.

Back at my parents' house, I don't park in the driveway, but as far out of the way as I can on a street-side parking pad. This is where I'll leave the car until I return, and I don't want it to be in the way of the aides' cars. I go inside to visit and to say goodbye to my dad. I have no idea how I will do this. I picture him in bed, me silently continuing to review if what we are saying to each other is enough, silently trying to think what I might say about my next visit and the car. Instead, I spend most of my time talking with my mom while my dad naps, finding conversation soothing as I wonder about saying that goodbye.

My dad wakes up, and I tell him which of my friends is coming to pick me up to drive me to the airport. He asks his aide to wheel him out of the bedroom so he can sit with me in the living room as I wait. The friend who is coming is among the most beautiful of all my friends, and my father likes pretty women. He lights up when she enters the room, her black curls framing her tanned Mediterranean complexion. Her hazel eyes engage his, still deep blue, as she tells him what a pleasure it is to see him again. I leave them visiting and find my mother to kiss her goodbye.

When I return to the living room to pick up my bag, I don't know how I am going to get through this moment. I kiss the top of my dad's head; I kiss him right beside the peg that covers the hole a surgeon made years before for an experimental procedure to reduce his tremors. I raise my lips and step back, seeing the sparkle in my mother's crystal lamp bases and bright orange blown glass, the deep green of the tall, broad-leafed philodendron by the side of the couch and the spiky cactus by a far window. I see the black of the wheelchair strident against the room's beige upholstery. How will we say goodbye?

With formality, my father puts his hand to his forehead in a salute and utters a soft, but resonant, "See ya."

That is when my heart breaks. He hasn't said, "See you in a couple of months," the way he usually acknowledges my next coming. Instead, he is letting me know he knows he won't be here. He never liked to see me cry, so I shed my tears after I close the door behind me.

At home in Los Angeles, I tell the support group I attend for parents who have lost grown children about my visit with my dad. When we light candles for our children and listen to one another talk about the hard parts of living without them, I am thinking about my father. When we stand in a circle holding hands at the end of the session, each of us connected in sadness and in strength—the strength it takes to get to the group, to admit fears and selfish thoughts of missing what our children could have done for us, of not being interested in much besides our bereavement, of annoyance with those around us whose insensitivity seems more than we can deal with—I think of my father. I think of his graciousness and bravery. I think of him looking at the picture of sun over Gold Lake breaking through playful orca clouds.

As I leave the group, I like the way the sun seems more brilliant when I walk to my parking spot down the street. If there are clouds from the West Los Angeles marine layer, the sun always breaks through. I count on this, the larger world making itself known to me.

I turn on my cell phone.

My mother has left me a message about their family physician making a house call and, after examining my dad, saying it is time to call Hospice. My father must know that Hospice nurses will come with morphine that will not only make him more comfortable now that his body's systems are failing, but also hasten a coma. My mother says that, after the doctor left, my father asked her to lie down beside him for a little while, not in her hospital bed like at night, but in his.

On May 6, 2001, when I leave my weekly grief support group, I find a message from Kurt. My sister called. My father is dead.

Within days, I am delivering a eulogy at the same synagogue where we so recently held services for Seth. My sister speaks about our father's tenacity in getting jobs done, even if he disliked the work he had to do—the bookshelves he built for her in one of her first apartments and the way, when we were teens, he painted the concrete posts of our basement recreation room with dragons. She tells the group that she hadn't really known he didn't like carpentry and painting, and that his enthusiasm, she learned years later, was only because he was doing it for his children.

I read words my mother prepared about a boy she had known since they were eleven, a boy who ate the note she passed him when the rabbi noticed them in Hebrew School, a teen who had been with her when her period came, a friend who had known what it was and what to do that afternoon at the Sutter Theater's Saturday matinee. Her love, her anchor has left before her. I know she sits there thinking that having said yes to Hospice, for the first time in her life *she* is the one who hurried *him* out the door. Perhaps the doctor was wrong. It is her what-if.

I turn to the writing I prepared and speak about words my father taught me. The years he was climbing the corporate ladder, he asked, "Do I look presentable?" He wouldn't leave the kitchen for the garage without our answer. "No man is indispensable" was his mantra, keeping him motivated toward excellence, but at the same time prepared for disappointment. I speak about other gifts I think he most enjoyed giving us—

copies of books like *Treasure Island*, a white football he tried to teach us to throw, a chemistry set we could use only with him as our proctor, the money we saved each week for college in a blue envelope we took to our school's special banking program. And I speak of the things I considered gifts—riding his shoulders to play at what seemed like great height in a swimming pool, his hand on the back of my two-wheeler seat as I pedaled down the sidewalk learning to balance, his driving lessons, the degree of attention and seriousness he gave the task and his bravery sitting with me as I pressed the accelerator. When I had my first job as an administrator and found the nonprofit I worked for was in the red, my father came to visit and sat for hours teaching me how to create, monitor, and control an organization's budget. When I had a collection of poems that needed presales for the small press to make a print run, my father ordered fifty copies and eventually gave them out like cigars when a baby is born. When Seth designed a house for me, my father paid for the skylights, an extra that would make all the difference to Seth's design, but one I couldn't afford.

I speak about a poem I wrote the year before he died, when I was writing exercises for a column on writing poetry. Thinking of how few Father's Day cards were left for me to send, I created an exercise for my readers to write Father's Day poems. I combed my memory for moments with my dad that could have been photographed. I thought about the days he bought that white football and tried teaching my sister and me to play. I thought about the way he stayed in his car doing paperwork before he came in at the end of his day, and how I watched him from the window. I thought about sitting in the back seat of the car when he taught my mother to parallel park between bushel baskets amidst colorful fall leaves.

The moment that inspired me to write, though, was a memory of him in our family room on Sunday nights, studying detail cards with information about pharmaceuticals to prepare sales talks for doctors he would call on that week. I remembered a rocking chair I sat in while I listened to him, and I gathered images from the evenings I'd been his audience while he practiced presentations. I wondered, "What do the activity and the images make me think about my father and our relationship?" The answer to that question became the poem's ending:

Sitting in the Black and Gold Replica of an Early American Rocker

I see my father at his maple desk staring at index
cards to memorize the pharmaceutical sales pitches
he'll need that week to call on doctors, his hair closely
cropped because it's barbered every Saturday. I know
his suit and tie hang neatly on the valet outside his closet.
When he gives me the cards he's studied so I can quiz
    him,
I think he stumbles just to test my knowledge and
    attention.
So much time before I know he makes mistakes at all.

And now, again, I don't believe he made mistakes. He found a way to let me know he was saying goodbye, a way to lend dignity to our anticipated and hard-to-bear parting.

My sister and I leave the bema to sit beside our mother. We stand when the rabbi leads the congregation in reciting Kaddish, the Jewish prayer for the dead.

"Yisgadal v'yiskadash sh'mei rabbaw. B'allmaw dee v'raw chir'usei," we chant, and then, "Yis'bawrach, v'yishtabach, v'yispaw'ar, v'yisromam, v'yis'nasei, v'yis'hadar, v'yis'aleh, v'yis'halawl sh'mei d'kudshaw b'rich hu."

"Blessed, praised, glorified, exalted, extolled, mighty, upraised, and lauded be the Name of the Holy One…beyond any blessing and song, praise and consolation that are uttered in the world. Now respond: Amen."

Four months ago, my father adamantly stood in honor of his grandson. *Blessed, praised, glorified, exalted, extolled, mighty, upraised.* The prayer is the sound of life pounded back into me.

Chapter Seven

Wedding Weekend

After a Great Love, 1983

Sometimes when oyster shells lie open
on the abandoned rowboat bleached from sun
and barnacles are heavy with mud in the salt marsh,
a loon yodels across the breeding waters
as I make my way through long, brown grass.

I sit in Kristen's parents' gracious family room off their kitchen. While Kurt and Bob talk outside in the garden, Jackie shows me photos of Seth.

"On his first Christmas here, Seth convinced me to let him make a chocolate brownie dessert to add to the desserts my caterer was supplying for a big party. I didn't want to interfere with what the caterers had planned. But Seth persisted in his desire to make something for the party, and I gave in."

I flinch, wondering what made Seth so insistent on doing things his way.

Jackie smiles. "Seth's brownies were the first to disappear when my guests started on dessert." The smile fades quickly. "I can't tell you how angry I am that Seth is gone. I am angry that I didn't do what I could have that day to keep him safe. If I hadn't stayed with visiting nieces and nephews, I would have skied with Seth, and he wouldn't have gone snowboarding.

"Or, maybe I could have convinced him to be a sweeper with me, to keep me company as I stayed behind the others to help any who fell and to keep out of the way of the faster ones. He would have, and he'd still be alive. Seth and I spoke early that morning about how neither one of us was actually in the mood to ski that day. He had a cold, and I was very tired from the holidays. I thought, if we stayed in for the day, he could sit by the fire while I assembled Christmas cards. Then Kris asked him to take it easy, too, to ski rather than snowboard. But he stuck with the snowboard plan."

I am not sure I'd ever thought that having a cold might have affected Seth's reflexes that day. I wished as hard as she did that any changes could have made a difference. I knew the loop of what-ifs, the way blaming oneself is logical when you can't explain how something could have happened to someone you love.

"I am angry. So angry," Jackie says. I think of my anger at Seth and Kristen's landlady that morning in the redwood grove for the way she trivialized Seth's spirit, implying that the way he wanted her to move garbage cans was silly.

Most of the time, something besides anger still takes over me, something connected to the orca clouds we'd seen the day we spread Seth's ashes at Gold Lake. I don't know what I can say here in Jackie's house amidst her memories and pictures of Seth that will help. I know that, beyond believing that Kristen had made a wonderful choice for her marriage partner, Jackie loved Seth and had taken him into her family. Kurt and I love Kristen and hope she'll always be a part of our lives. Anger will not help us hold onto the people Seth loved, to the people who can help us know more of him now. I am eager to share the poem and the photo Kurt and I brought.

Everyone reads the poem. We smile, remembering the shirt Seth wore. Jackie tells us about the dress shoes Seth left in their house when they flew to Breckenridge.

"When we flew back to Kansas City to get ready to go to Seattle, I found his shoes carefully placed outside the guest room closet door. I knew he'd done that to remember them when he and Kris came back to Kansas City from Colorado before heading back to Berkeley, since airfares were cheaper that way. I moved the shoes into the guestroom closet—barely. When I'm overwhelmed with sadness or worried about Kristen, I have long conversations with the shoes, as if Seth were standing in them and listening."

Now I begin to wonder how she and Bob have handled many things. What have they done with the beautiful wedding dress they purchased for Kristen? How did they find the strength to pay attention to things like canceling the reservation for the June weekend at Gold Mountain? They had already made a down payment. I wonder if invitations had been ordered and printed.

These things seem too mundane, too small to talk about. Seth, whom Kristen loved, whom Jackie and Bob and Kristen's sisters loved, who was supposed to be marrying Kristen and leaving on a honeymoon within a few days, is not here. We are all enlisting memories of the past to keep us going, but only Kristen and her parents have had to deal with the practical logistics of canceling a future.

I hope Kristen will see the magic in the picture of Gold Lake when we spread Seth's ashes. I hope it will help over the months as she mourns the wedding she was looking forward to, the day she would have exchanged vows surrounded by wildflowers.

I imagine Seth dressed for his wedding, almost comfortable in the white summer suit he decided to wear. I picture the men at the wedding weekend, including Seth, fly fishing in the lake, each fish caught and released like a prayer for a happy life, many children, prosperity. I feel the cool spring Colorado mountain air I knew from visits, hear the words of the ceremony, "I do," the traditional stomping of the wine glass at a Jewish wedding, "L'Chiam. To life."

In the Kansas humidity and heat, I conjure the event that has been amputated from our lives, a phantom wedding. I remember that people who have had amputations report feeling their missing limbs. In fact, I have read, those born without limbs sometimes say they have sensations from limbs they never had. I will always feel this wedding I never attended. But I know I will also feel the amazing sense of divinity that rushed in when we brought Seth's ashes to the wedding site.

In the evening, at a long table on the outdoor patio of a neighborhood restaurant, we all settle into a way of talking about the past and the future. Kristen tells Kurt and me about the attic she took over as a teenager, and the way her younger sister loved it now. We listen to stories of her roller-skating in the big empty downstairs of the house when her family first moved into it. We wonder what college her younger sister, Caitlin, will select, and we talk about Kristen's upcoming year, traveling on a grant she applied for to research squatters' villages all over the world to see what architects might bring to the areas.

We know she applied for the grant so she could take her sorrow to places where sorrow runs deep. She would not have to think about where she wanted to live in the future. She could stay the way she was now. Exploring the world's squatters' villages, places where drug overdoses and drug deals gone bad kill people, where disease and famine keep loss knocking daily on everyone's door, she would make her sorrow indistinguishable from that of humanity. She would keep herself from feeling too much of the phantom life. Love is a ladder to the divine, the Sufis say. Its base, I realize, can be placed anywhere.

After dinner, Jackie and Kristen show Kurt and me the house's original kitchen, hidden but still intact behind the new walls of the remodel. Completely functional, the kitchen is cherished by the family; the happy memories and times remain even as family members move forward. As we sit in the family room off the new kitchen and talk about the way Kristen and Seth jumped right into the remodel planning with their newly minted ideas, I concentrate on that original kitchen. Just like Kristen's memory of the empty house she roller-skated in, just like the original kitchen untouched behind all that was new, Seth will remain in Kristen's life and the life of her family, in my life and in the life of my family, nurturing the good times, supporting us in the difficult ones. We'll grow older, but our love for Seth and his for us will be at the heart of our houses.

Kristen and Seth had been together for years. They were ready to invite family and friends to honor their commitment. All unions, even those that end, are eternally inside each partner. Someday, when Kristen commits to another partner, I know she will feel the continuing presence of Seth's love and her love for him. Love doesn't erase itself, after all; it expands.

As we tour Kansas City the next day, we note cow sculptures on the many blocks we walk. They are for sale in an auction to raise money for the city. I think of the angel sculptures all over Los Angeles, also intended to raise funds. In Kansas City, cows from this world, and in Los Angeles, angels from the other—both offered for sustenance, art become bread. I walk with Kristen through the streets of Kansas City and think about transformation. In the wedding ceremony she and Seth had planned, they would each have held a candle and used it to light another to symbolize two souls becoming one.

Seth is dead, but his love for Kristen doesn't seem at all like a candle snuffed out. It seems like a candle burning invisibly, like the sun when night comes. Kristen is flung to the far reaches of herself, but she has the light of this union, of being so deeply loved, to take with her. Orcas spend their lives traveling with their families. The life of what could have been and the life Kristen is bravely preparing to embark on are wed and exist together.

I write this poem for her:

I Remember Gold Mountain
For Kristen Belt

Seth is not here for you
to walk to, to light
the candle of your joining.
Guests are not in outdoor
seats overlooking
lake and stone.

But I remember Gold Mountain
when I spread
his ashes five months ago
beneath a winter shrub
closest to the altar site
that you described.

Sun broke through
just then, brought warmth
that overrode the cold,
transformed clouds to orcas,
and there were two
jumping over an orb of light.

The last full day of our visit, Bob invites Sonny and Kurt to
play golf. Jackie knows of my interest in shamans and has made
appointments for us to see a woman she's heard of. Kristen
joins us for lunch. She doesn't want an appointment, but when
I ask her if she ever feels that Seth is with her, she tells me about
her hours in studio, the way her skill at doing drawings has
increased quickly, progressing through many levels, as if Seth,
who was very good at studio work, is guiding her hand.

The woman we see tells me that Seth felt compelled not to get a helmet the day of his accident. Something was drawing him despite his earthly good sense. I don't think Kristen would have liked hearing that, but it confirms what I believe. She tells Jackie that Kristen will have children and, in pictures of her family, a globe of light behind everyone will show Seth's presence. Perhaps that image would be more welcome to Kristen, softer, more earthbound.

As traveler, Kristen will do what Jackie and I are doing that afternoon: giving in, with the help of messages and images, to the conditions life has imposed on us, locating a place where the work of healing can happen.

I can honor the right conversations, whether they are with poets and authors I find in print or with people I meet along the way who speak a language I need to immerse myself in. I remember words from "Dreams in Dialogue" by the Spanish poet, Antonio Machado:

Oh solitude, my sole companion,
muse of marvels, that gave my voice
the word unasked for, answer my question!
Who is this now with whom I talk?

Our divine selves, connection to all that is, will arrive whether we are talking to shamans or to empty shoes, to sunlight or to squatters; these are muses and our healing, the ones that break through infinity and bring always. Machado describes it in his poem, "Passageways":

The row of gleaming windows
holds a twin cameo profile
repeated through the silver glass.
Who is it that has pierced time's heart?

That night, Kurt and I lie in the guest room bed, talking. He tells me that the course he played that afternoon with Bob and Sonny is the oldest one he has ever been on.

"Kansas City's history is rough," he says, "before and after the Civil War. And a lot of what is here now was built with Mob money. But even with all the corruption and war in the city's history, here we were, today, playing on a course that felt like an ode to civilization. It made me think of higher selves, the best in humans."

How is it an ode? I wonder.

"The fairways are wide. People can't hit into each other's way. The whole design seems to create tolerance. There are hundred-year-old trees on the course, but they aren't hazards. They're an amazing backdrop. The grace in the environment is so strong, I think it makes everyone on the course focus on being civilized.

"As we went from hole to hole, I imagined telling Seth the feelings I was having. I wished he were there with me to explain the way the design of the course made me feel the way I did. I wanted to walk the course with him. And suddenly I knew how much he would have loved the years ahead, dipping into Kristen's family's elegant home base," Kurt says softly and kisses me goodnight.

He has described what I aspire to in my grieving. The joy I can find in a world without Seth will have to be built on tolerance. It needs beauty and grace to protect it. It has to honor the extraordinary, as well as the mundane. And it is a jewel purchased with the wages of turmoil.

CHAPTER EIGHT

ENDLESSLY ROCKING

Foggy Afternoon in Cambridge, 1992

Ambulance in Harvard Square, a young woman
hugging her guy, his smashed green sedan
hitched to a tow truck, a crowd gathered thick
as the one last night for street musicians.
Then, my mother-in-law's weeping on our voice mail
as she reports a car crash in her town, the death
of her neighbor's daughter and granddaughter.
I sigh under the salty fog. Starlings fly
like pieces of brown earth crumbling. If I breathe
fog, will some of the sea begin to move inside me?

Mid-June, I begin preparations for the annual Colorado Mountain Writers' Workshop that I teach with two colleagues. As faculty, we lead workshops during the day and read to our students from our own work in the evenings. My interior life has changed so drastically that only my new poems seem suitable to me to read, and I wish to have more of them.

I turn again to Edward Hirsch's book hoping to make another assignment for myself. This time, I gravitate toward his discussion of Walt Whitman and the use of sound in his poem, "Out of the Cradle Endlessly Rocking." Hirsch writes that this poem is a "lullaby of sadness that permeates the very universe itself," "a lullaby that moves from chanting to singing." In this poem, he believes, Whitman "had become a shaman" who would "author a reminiscence for us," "summon up experience in us."

Nothing can match my needs more than to read this lullaby of sadness and author my own reminiscence to summon up experience.

"Out of all potential words, these words alone; out of all potential memories, this memory alone," Hirsch incants. "The rhetorical rhythm of lines [urges] fundamental memory to issue forth."

I seek fundamental memories of my son. I cannot seek enough of them.

In the early morning light, I read and re-read Whitman's poem:

Out of the Cradle Endlessly Rocking

Out of the mocking-bird's throat, the musical shuttle.
Out of the Ninth-month midnight,
Over the sterile sands, and the fields beyond, where the
    child, leaving his bed, wander'd alone, bare-headed,
    barefoot,
Down from the shower'd halo,
Up from the mystic play of shadows, twining and
    twisting as if they were alive,
Out from the patches of briers and blackberries,
From the memories of the bird that chanted to me,
From your memories, sad brother—from the fitful
    risings and fallings I heard,
From under that yellow half-moon, late-risen, and
    swollen as if with tears,
From those beginning notes of sickness and love, there
    in the transparent mist,
From the thousand responses of my heart, never to
    cease,
From the myriad thence-arous'd words,
From the word stronger and more delicious than any,
From such, as now they start, the scene revisiting,
As a flock, twittering, rising, or overhead passing,
Borne hither—ere all eludes me, hurriedly,
A man—yet by these tears a little boy again,
Throwing myself on the sand, confronting the waves,
I, chanter of pains and joys, uniter of here and hereafter,
Taking all hints to use them—but swiftly leaping
    beyond them,
A reminiscence sing.

It is easy to chastise myself for what little I remember each day compared to how many years Seth was here. But writing the villanelle, "A New Theology," after dreaming of Seth in a garden has already taught me that the state between action and dreaming is where knowledge and acceptance lie. I trust that whatever memories come are the right ones for me to chant and, in the act of chanting, I'll sing a resurrection of my boy.

For awhile, I concentrate on Whitman's ending, reading and re-reading it until I believe I can become a "uniter of here and hereafter":

> Throwing myself on the sand, confronting the waves,
> I, chanter of pains and joys, uniter of here and hereafter,
> Taking all hints to use them—but swiftly leaping
>   beyond them,
> A reminiscence sing.

I have been throwing myself for months now on the shores of my grief, at the beach between here and hereafter. Now I dedicate myself to using Whitman's pattern for learning how to unite them.

Somehow, the memories that come are not of Seth's infancy or younger years. I am seeing him clearly as an upper classman at the University of Colorado. I remember him noticing how out of breath I am on hikes when I visit. I see Seth taking off with Kurt ahead of me, tackling the steepest parts of trails. I hear Seth laughing at me for not noticing that I was huffing because of the altitude. Under the influence of Whitman and Hirsch's discussion, my images of Seth flow into form and center on his activity with college friends:

Six Months after My Son's Death,
I Chant to Sing for Him

Out of daily steps and out of drives
on highways, out of hours' rocky patches
and moments made of weeds, memories come.

I sing the evening I visited my son and watched
his friends working in his kitchen with hops and yeast
and recipes downloaded from the Internet.
I sing the carboys they showed me topped
with see-through tubes and shiny copper
for reading yeast's performance.

I sing their logs of sugar content and bottled
batches, the way the young men sterilized the bottles
they used, invited people for the harvests
of oatmeal stout and porter. I sing each week
they went to school between their Sunday fests.
Long and deep, I mourn and wake to sing the sun
to rise, to thank my son for time he's spent
inside my dreams. I sing, I sing and do what
he was doing, siphoning good spirit from sediment.

During the days I am in Colorado to teach, I walk to town
on my time off between lectures and workshops, and every-
where I see young men dressed in the kind of clothes Seth wore
during his brewing days, their flannel shirts unbuttoned, white
tee shirts showing through. I drive to an aspen grove to hear
the tree leaves clap, as I did the day I hiked with Seth, and he
had me listen to the sound of them.

When it is my turn to give an evening reading, I share the poems I have written since Seth died, believing in the need for poets to be honest, to share what is in them to write. Over the next days of the conference, people hand me poems and essays about losses in their lives, about what it means to experience mine with me. Betty, who has come to our conference for two years, tells me she lost her forty-year-old son the year before we met. She shows me writing that came when she returned to her room after my reading. It begins:

> Until I heard a poem written by a mother who lost her grown son, I couldn't write about John. While the poet spoke of happy times and a great loss, I cried for hours and searched my thoughts for something to say. Where are the happy memories?
>
> John died on my birthday almost three years ago. The coroner said it was an accident, that he took street and prescription drugs until they stopped his heart. I'm not sure.

Doris, a cancer survivor from Australia, hands me a poem the next morning. She worried that perhaps she was overstepping bounds, but she wants me to know the feelings she's had listening to me:

> How can I mourn a boy who lives?
> his love reflects from her eyes
> his embrace hugs her shoulders
> his breath moves her hair
> as his mother tells her story
>
> I feel that I already knew him.

I have taught many times that the power of poetry is in its ability to transmit experience directly without going through the head, but through the senses. I am grateful to learn that I have brought Seth to life for others, that what I wrote convinces others Seth is with me and persuades them to risk the pain of evoking their loss so they can remember more of their lives with the deceased. What we see, smell, taste, touch, and hear provides experience we live and relive. What is the quality in the experience I share that makes many of those who listen immediately write? I feel no overstepping of bounds, just love stepping into my days.

Karen writes that she lost a baby:

She was my gift as your son was yours and is. I know you know this. I saw it in your eyes when you read of Seth's life, its passing, and the wounds your writing is helping you to bind. Forgive me for leaving as I listened; there is a place in my heart where memories of Sarah live. Your words drew me there. Thank you.

How brave you are to share such sadness with strangers. I will tell you that grieving your child is a long, long journey. I hope you bring lots of pens and keep writing.

Pat hands me a letter saying that she, like Doris, felt my son's presence in the room as I read:

Your Seth was much with us. I had no sense of an image, a gray fog or a light. He hovered tall on your left side, solicitous and leaning. I get the sense that Seth very much wants to help your healing. He is still very much part of your life—not in the gone but not forgotten sense—but in the way it was when he was away from home. Sheila, no one who's not lost a child can know the searing scour of the heart or the numb voice of the brain after such a loss. But my heart does hurt with yours. And I will be a writer. Because I see you very definitely have proven to me the power and worth of writing.

Poetry is helping me find out how the loss of Seth can bring me to him. I am letting him drive me around and around, so I can write poetry, and it is helping people talk.

I arrive home from the writers' conference and dump my books, papers, pens, group photos, and Steamboat tourist information onto my sunlit desk. Looking at the pile of stuff on the desk reminds me of an afternoon I'd picked Seth up at the house of one of his schoolmates. I found my son in the family's large dining room, playing with his friend. A huge pile of toys, art supplies, and clothes, with silverware poking out here and there, lined the length of a back wall. The pile came out from the wall at least a foot and was three feet high. I was horrified to see such disorder. When I asked Seth if it felt weird to have that big mess in the room where he was playing and having an afternoon snack, he said, "No, it's kind of fun. Whenever you get bored, you just go to the pile for something new."

I pluck something from the pile of paper I've made before me on the desk. It is the one older poem that I took to the conference to read at one of my workshops. I wrote it six months before Seth's accident, as I was creating a lesson for my July poetry column and wanted to experiment with the effects of copying the poetic strategy of the United States Declaration of Independence. At the time, I was already enthralled with Hirsch's words, especially these on repetition:

> ...words accumulate mysterious power and resonance through repetition. Anaphora serves as an organizing poetry strategy for long lists or catalogs, and the piling up of particulars is itself a joyous poetic activity, a way of naming and claiming the world.

I had decided to examine what would happen if I declared my independence from the art I believed had empowered me to see who I was:

Poetry

> You have refused to come to me when I have called you
>   directly,
> You have come joking in a fool's chiming rhymes when
>   you did appear,
> You have dropped phrases here and there leaving me to
>   find the puzzle they complete,
> You have distracted me from living the way others think I
>   ought to,
> You have ignited desire in me when boredom was the
>   companion I thought I preferred,
> You have made me cry in public and you have left me
>   speechless in front of students,
> You have come to me unbidden in the mail, on bus
>   placards and city steps,

hooking me and reeling me in until I flutter and gasp,
You have made me search you out in books I'd never
    heard of,
You have made me a lover of frogs in ancient China,
a collector of words I like the sound of like anticubital.
You have widened my circle of friends to old men in Chile
    and young girls in Greece.
And you have made as foreigners those closer to home
    who don't understand the calling.
I have reminded you that I must earn a living,
I have asked you to wait so I can sleep, rolling away from
    the pad and lighted pen,
I have turned my head because I was lazy watching
    television or reading Sunday's *Parade*
I have sometimes committed to organizations hoping
    deadlines and databases would keep you away,
I have refused to watch a sunrise, forgotten to walk by the
    ocean, not named
the feel of a dolphin's skin.
I have turned your corners down like hotel bed sheets and
    never returned.
Yet there are no vows that I can break with you, my fated
    life companion,
you who come to me sometimes hidden under armor and
    sometimes naked in a waterfall,
you who come to me in a peasant's apron as well as a
    queen's robe and crown,
you who are as afraid of light as rock crabs and as agile
    sighted as eagles,
you who are as unpluckable as shooting stars and
    harvested as pinion nuts,

you who are as ethereal as the ocean's spindrift, as
muscular as undertow.

Anaphora, Hirsh says in a discussion of the tools of repeti-
tion, means a carrying back to carry forward. Using it whips
the ends of poetry lines to the start of new ones, keeps the
writer and reader moving on down the page with momentum.

When I wrote the poem, "Poetry," I smiled at the length of
the lines in my declaration. One of my very first teachers, the
poet David Wagoner, warned me about a tendency to "reduce
myself to a laconic whisper." I had been a very shy child. I
didn't like to talk to people I didn't know, and I didn't like to
talk to people I couldn't see, like our town's telephone operator
before we had dial tones. Poems were like speaking to someone
I couldn't see. It was hard to get the words out. I was afraid I
would fail to please the person who waited to hear from me.
But David Wagoner had encouraged me to speak with range,
to use long lines, to cry out as well as to whisper.

"I'm a bubble, I'm a bubble, I'm a bubble," my father sug-
gested I say to myself when I was in junior high school. He said
I should repeat this phrase over and over, because I wouldn't
be able to remain withdrawn if I were saying it. And he dem-
onstrated by sitting across from me, popping up and down on
his seat while he chanted, "I'm a bubble, I'm a bubble, I'm a
bubble."

I see him now, sitting there, raising his shoulders each time
he says, "I'm" and puffing out his cheeks after he says, "a bub-
ble." My father won me over with this comic repetition.

Smiling at the memory, I feel something like the sea
moving inside me. As ethereal as spindrift and as muscular
as undertow, poetry made possible my connections to self, to

others, and to learning what seems beyond understanding. I feel gratitude to each poem I have written and to each one I have read. I learn from writing poems that I can never be independent from poetry. Now that I've relied on poems to help me grieve, I know for sure this art is stronger than I am, longer lasting than my ability to ignore it from time to time. I am not nearly as shy as I was when my father offered me his refrain.

CHAPTER NINE

THE VEIL

Point Reyes, 1979

Where land bellies toward the ocean
you walk imported as the Scotch broom.
You know the lesson: take root
with fennel and tan oak,
among bay laurel and sage.
Take root like succulents under blue sky.
Meadows here are bowls for the wind swirl.
Rest.

When you can, find the Farallons
like whales in a distance no longer tolerable.
Let loose ends lead to their own ends.
Stand by the ocean loving what is temporary,
the day's work of tide pools, gull prints in sand,
what lashes in like lizards, like legend,
like the light in this day.

In August, I make another trip back to the Port Townsend house Seth designed. I find a letter I left on my desk. It was written by a man I consider a spiritual guide. I had asked him about the sun that day at Gold Mountain. "Oh, Sheila, the sun is the giver of life and the receiver of death," he wrote. "The sun is the beginning and the end of an octave." He added words from *Beelzebub's Tales to His Grandson* by George Ivanovitch Gurdjieff, a man who looked to ancient traditions to understand the meaning of human life: "The most holy sun absolute where our Lord sovereign endlessness has the fundamental place of his dwelling."

I looked up the word "octave": the interval of eight diatonic degrees between two tones of the same name, the higher of which has twice as many vibrations per second as the lower. I read that the human ear tends to hear notes an octave apart as essentially the same. Birth and death, the anchors of our individual octaves. In being here to experience Seth's death, as I was at his birth, I have the opportunity to believe and to live the idea that his new higher vibration is something I can't hear, but can feel. "I will drive you around and around," Seth said. "You and Seth have been together before in many lives," the first shaman said. Villanelles circle loss to retrieve it because holding it is important. All these months, the images I responded to were about the way lives are cradled by endlessness.

I pick up *Duino Elegies*, a translation of Rainer Maria Rilke's poetry I had left on my desk next to the letter. I remember that I had found the poems comforting in the way that the music of words comforts me, even if I can't concentrate on meaning. Now, I lay the letter down and open the book of poems from the back, remembering how my spiritual guide told me that he opened all books as if they were Hebrew books, reading back to front. I stop on the pages of Rilke's eighth elegy. In it, he seems to me to be writing about the "sovereign endlessness" that Gurdjieff named:

> Never for one day do we
> turn from forms to face
> that place of endless purity
> blooming flowers forever know.
> Always a world for us, never
> the nowhere minus the no:
> that innocent, unguarded
> space which we could breathe,
> know endlessly, and never require.
> A child, at times, may lose
> himself within the stillness
> of it, until rudely ripped away.
> Or one dies and IS the place.
> As death draws near,
> one sees death no more, rather
> looks beyond it with, perhaps,
> the broader vision of the beasts.

I turn again to the letter on my desk:

I have the strong impression that Seth's essence and his personality were well-balanced, consequently, his life, short in our usual thinking, was in fact far longer than is usual simply because so many impressions were received directly in his essence. This doesn't happen to most of us because our personalities are so strong they block impressions from touching us deeply. And essence is buried very deep.

Something, I don't know what or who, tells me that Seth is all right. Something knows something. That is probably the extent of my knowledge. And that is my search.

I leave the letter open on my desk as I continue thumbing backwards through the book of Rilke's elegies. In "The Seventh Elegy," I read:

> Each of you had her hour,
> or if not an hour,
> an instant, at least,
> between two moments when
> life burst into flower.
> Every blessed petal.
> Your veins throbbed with it.
> But we so soon forget what
> our laughing neighbor neither
> applauds nor envies.
> We desire that they be admired,
> but even the most visible
> of joys cannot be seen
> until transformed—within.
> Nowhere, beloved, does any
> world exist save that within.
> Life spends itself in
> the act of transformation,
> dissolving, bit by bit,
> the world as it appeared.

I actually felt impressions of endlessness directly for "an instant, at least, / between two moments..." when I brought my son's ashes to the ground I knew he wanted to stand upon. My "veins throbbed with it" again when I sat with Kristen at the Synagogue, readying for Seth's funeral services, and sun seemed suddenly to break through a hall window to shine on us. I felt it the day of the family ceremony at Discovery Bay as we returned the rest of Seth's ashes to the world. The grey sky had again broken open with sun. I felt sun flow into my veins when I walked on my way to a first meeting of the grief support group I was hesitant about joining. And I felt it each morning, when I watched the new sun in the sky. These moments were very brief, but they were direct.

"Something knows something." This must be, I think, what Rilke means by "nowhere minus the no". I leaf further from back to front in Rilke's elegies. I stop this time at "The First Elegy":

> Children who have gone do not require us.
> Weaned, they need no mother's breast.
> Our joys and sorrows don't concern them.
> But *we*, for whom the mysteries are golden,
> still unsolved, our very sustenance—
> can we exist without *them*?

Before he was two, I thought, Seth had weaned from my breast, eager to go on and explore life. I realize that now I have to wean myself from wanting to see him in his life's quandaries and ecstasies: which job to take and, before that, when to marry Kristen and, before that, which graduate school to attend and, before that, whether to be on a mountain biking team and, before that, which college to choose and, before that, how to build sets for the school plays and the mock trial courtroom and, before that, whether to go to the grocery store with me or stay home watching TV and, before that, how to know it was his play on the soccer field and, before that, how to tell us he thought kisses had germs. Instead of wishing to add to the list from the top down, now I have to let Seth enter into my life from my memories. I have to wean myself from wanting to see him alive in earthly joys and sorrows. I have to let in whatever comes of him apropos of the present.

"Do you think?" he always said if I told him what I thought he might consider when he hadn't yet made up his mind.

When Seth weaned from my breast, he didn't wean from my love. I won't wean from his or from the love I feel for him. I can give up future stages in our lives together on earth without giving up love. Seth taught me how he did it when he gave up the breast, hadn't he? "Do you think?" I say to him.

Having finished my journey reading from back to front, I thumb forward to Rilke's "The Tenth Elegy." Here I find something more that I need:

> Were the endlessly dead
> to awaken some symbol,
> within us, to indicate
> themselves, they might
> point to the catkins
> dangling from the leafless
> branches of the Hazel trees.
> Or speak in drops of rain
> falling to dark earth
> in early spring.
>
> Then we,
> who have known joy

only as it escapes us,
rising to the sky,
would receive the
overwhelming benediction
of happiness descending.

When Emily was very young, maybe three, she described a dream she'd had. She said, "Mommy ran like raindrops and floated up to the sky. She hung her umbrella up on a cloud and fell back down to earth, watering the flowers." My daughter told me then that, when happiness falls, it graces those of us below.

I leave the book and the letter on my desk and go outside to the garden in front of the house to pull sorrel and crab grass from the damp earth under moon yarrow. I delight in finding stray California poppies and orange calendula under the rockroses, small juniper, and pines. Creeping thyme covers the pathways, and I breathe its fragrance as I rest on the steps to my deck. Then I pace the deck, back and forth, between its covered and uncovered portions. This house is alive with my son and my son's spirit. His art is here, not only the photographs he took and the picture frames he made in woodshop and the rendering he drew in an architecture class, but his esthetic is also in the balance of room proportions and dimensions: the window placement, the gentle roof, the setback from the street.

To my mind, he sits afternoons in the hammock as he did each summer home from college. Evenings, he settles with me on our cedar chairs to watch the sun set, and mornings I hear him taking his kayak out from the crawl space under the house. I know that, in the phantom life, he pulls the kayak down to the beach on the little set of wheels he put together, then paddles quietly out toward the Olympics, turning right toward North Beach and the Strait of Juan de Fuca. His hair is sun-streaked, his arms tanned and strong. He laughs at my worries and tells me I did a good job of raising him and must trust him. And I know whatever compelled Seth to snowboard on that day without a helmet, whatever happened on that run at Breckenridge, is bigger than his earthly presence. Believing that is as necessary to me now as breathing. I must trust him. I don't know how I know that, only that something knows something.

A few hours after I fall into a deep sleep, the light of the almost full moon wakes me. I go outside to look at it and find the sky covered with clouds, but somehow the moon appears to be in front of the quilted sheet of them. I look and I look and I look again. Still, it appears the moon is glowing in front of the clouds and, behind the moon, clouds are bright from the moonlight, like a curtain behind a bulb.

"Light what is veiled," I think, and I repeat words I memorized from the Prechtel interview in *The Sun*: "A shaman is someone who deals with the problems that arise when we forget the relationship that exists between us and the other world that feeds us, or when, for whatever reason, we don't feed the other world in return."

I will feed my son with what he never weaned himself from—my love and my gratitude for his time here with me. This is my sustenance, the food that needed sowing and harvesting. I could not merely snatch this food from the platters that many served up to me. The small yellow fish and the stars have to take up residence inside; they have to be ingested into every cell of the body. To feed your dead, you must metabolize the world.

CHAPTER TEN

CARRY BACK TO CARRY FORWARD

Missing You

In California, Manzanita, Spanish
for little apples, edges of the round
leaves pointing toward sun, shed
light, which is extravagant here.

I sit by a stream, watch water
come to a rock taller than the streambed,
watch its creases behind the rock,
the familiar swirl of fingerprints.

I lift my hand as if to let my fingers
move over the familiar terrain of you
when they move in this sun-warmed sand.

Two and a half years after Seth died, right after I teach another yearly Colorado Mountain Writers' Conference, I make a visit to my cousin Marion in Denver before I head home. As I carry my luggage down the steep steps to her guest room, tears choke my throat. I swallow hard and glance into the bathroom at the glazed shower stall. I stood in that stall sobbing, went up those steps on my way to the mortuary, sat in the room next door with Kurt, emailing our friends and relatives.

The last time I stayed here, I had come from the hospital, where I walked in and out of the room where Seth lay, his brain dead upon impact with a tree, his body an altar to which we brought our love.

For two summers following Seth's death, on the way to Steamboat Springs for the annual writers' conference, I had driven on highway 70 past the turnoff to Breckenridge, where he collided with that tree, and I never wanted to see the ski resort. This summer, on our way from the airport to Steamboat, I asked Jack, the colleague I was driving with, if we might take that detour.

We drove past the Breckenridge Nordic Center and on up to the ski lifts. In the early summer afternoon, we traveled along Sky Hill Road and turned on (can it be?) Shock Hill Drive. Two and a half years after my son died, I was at Cold Camp II. Near a sign for Peak Eight Village, Lift #7, Lift #5, Peaks 8, 9, and 7 and a children's ski school, I stood under a gentle breeze and sketched what I saw, so I could check with Kristen or the ski patrol's report to find out if I was anywhere near the accident.

When we were back on the road, Jack's cell phone rang. I listened to his side of the conversation and the pauses between his questions.

"Hi, Nick." Jack smiled. "How'd your game go today?"

"Pitched the first two?"

"Third base, and then you sat one?"

"Center. They didn't even get a fifth inning in the field? Who gave up all the runs?"

The third baseman had caught the ball, and Jack's son was out. He'd hurt his leg.

"You bandaged it?"

I did not bandage hurt, I thought, as we drove away from the ski area. Instead, I let lines of poetry confirm what I was coming to believe. There is peace at the center of everything. This world and another are joined.

In the days after the conference, I sit on the couch in Marion's family room and remember all of us gathered there, at her insistence, after the angiogram results that confirmed no blood had gotten to Seth's brain since the initial impact, after we'd given permission to harvest his organs, after we had a Rabbi lead us in prayer, after we had each touched his cheek and his hands, after we had kissed him. There must have been food, but I don't remember it. What I remember is lying on that couch, my voice so faint I didn't recognize it.

My daughter came and put her hand on my forehead. She said, "Mom, I want you to know that Vijay and I are planning on having children." She was doing more than dropping her annoyance at me, the potential grandmother, hinting despite myself; she was finding a way to deal with our family's loss, a way to honor what her brother had wanted in his own life.

Kristen came to sit by me, too. With all the strength I could muster, I spoke to her. "You know that Seth wanted more than anything to see you graduate from architecture school. If you can at all stay in the program, I think you should. I know your parents want to take care of you back at home. But think about what you were trying to accomplish. Think about continuing your life, if you can. I love you." We held each other's hand.

As I visit now, two and a half years later, Kristen is finishing work with an architecture firm in Rio de Janeiro, and Emily has given the family what she calls its "next good news" with the birth of her son, Toby. Marion's husband, Ira, asks how I can come back to Colorado at all. I tell him that I like to be in the landscape my son loved when he attended school here and learned about the Rockies. When I admit that I got sad on my way to the guest room, he immediately asked if I would rather stay in a different room. "No," I assure him. "I want to be there. I want to remember."

Later that evening, Marion and Ira's Portuguese Waterdog, Nolie, stays on my bed. She licks at a bug bite on my calf that I have scratched into a swollen ring of angry red. I know Nolie is protecting me. Dogs lick wounds to clean the dead skin away, to keep the circulation working, I've heard. When I awake in the morning, Nolie is still at the bottom of my bed. After I take a shower and return to the room to dress, she is there. She is there as I write notes about what I dreamt, sleeping in that guest room bed: Kurt was teaching writing to my students in my absence. Trying to be thorough, he was about to read an abundance of essays to the students. They seemed restless.

"I think it is time for a break," I said, suddenly entering the room. "Everyone take a half-hour."

The feeling of my intrusion into the classroom stays with me. I note that, though I worry that others outside of writing audiences grow restless if I speak of my feelings too often, Kurt is there whenever I feel sad, whenever I miss Seth. Kurt's thoroughness in wanting to include so many essays for the students let me know that there was always room in my life to remember Seth, not only in his perfection, but also in his foibles. I know Kurt and I can remind each other about the evening Seth served everyone at our table extremely slender pieces of a cherry pie he had made, either believing it was so good that a little went a long way or, more likely, wanting to save half the pie for himself. I know we can remember the summer just before he turned thirteen, when he slept and watched TV so much, we didn't understand where our energetic boy had gone. I know we could talk about the times as a young teen he had thought his mother suddenly the stupidest person on the planet, unable even to talk to a grocery store checker appropriately. I know we can remember the times he went off to help what seemed like scores of his friends when we had asked him to help us prepare for houseguests. Even remembering the difficult times, like the one when he unflatteringly mimicked the way I speak while a poetry publisher was with us at our dinner table, I am able to believe Kurt when he says my relationship with Seth was complete.

"Before he died, you fulfilled your parenting contract," Kurt says, "and Seth was grateful and launched into the world successfully."

I'd done my job well, like the shaman had said Seth wanted me to know. I can hold on to that.

I write more notes in the guest room. I am without my glasses, which I lost on the last day of the Steamboat conference. An attendee, a clinical psychologist, told me I must not have wanted to see my way home. I agree. I want to feel my way home, to the home inside me where I accept Seth's death, honor it, and move filled with love inspired by him. "I learn by going where I have to go," Theodore Roethke wrote in "The

Waking":

> What falls away is always. And is near.
> I wake to sleep, and take my waking slow.
> I learn by going where I have to go.

I glance at my open suitcase where a red shirt lies at the top of my clothes. It is oddly folded and round as a strawberry. I think of the afternoon I went with conference participants to visit Strawberry Hot Springs and soaked in three pools fed by springs and river water. I asked those soaking near me if they lived in Steamboat. "I do," said a man about my son's age. He had moved from Wisconsin for the snowboarding and said he loved Steamboat. He looked like my son, something about his hair and the color of his eyes, and the gentle way he spoke with a middle-aged woman. But it wasn't until he swam away nearer to young women that I realized it was as if Seth had visited for a moment.

I think about the evening before, when one of my students knocked on my door to ask if she could come by early the next morning to help me search for the glasses I'd lost. When she saw my purple eyeglass case on the desk in my room, she asked if she could open it, saying she believed "the eyeglasses might come home if we opened their house." In the guest room, I wrote:

That morning before traveling, I rose at six to meet Morgan in the hopes of finding my glasses, but also in the hopes of seeing the foxes so many others had reported all week. We stood outside in the early sunlight and shadows, staring at the embankment where we'd heard others had seen the foxes. Morgan pointed out the ridge above it where she'd seen them a few times that week. Nobody there. We walked down the road to get a cup of coffee at the school cafeteria and, as we came to the end of the embankment, I looked back over my shoulder. I saw movement on the ridge. "They are coming," I told her. And we watched a male and a female descend to the road. We were very near them, and they watched us watching them. Then they traveled past us, their silver, black, and auburn fur gleaming.

I remember that, when the foxes came, Morgan exclaimed, "Mother likes to show off her children." Every time I see Seth in someone else's posture and expression, Mother must be showing him to me, I think. I continue writing, Nolie still on my bed. Morgan was right about Mother Nature. But I guess my glasses weren't ready to come home. With my plane ride to Los Angeles still a few hours away, I use magnifiers I find at Marion's to search the teaching materials I have in my briefcase. I want poems about foxes. I don't have any, so I begin reading some of *In Jubilate Agno*, by Christopher Smart, who paid close attention to his cat in the 1700s:

For I Will Consider My Cat Jeoffrey

For he is the servant of the Living God, duly and daily
   serving him.
For at the first glance of the glory of God in the East he
   worships in his way.
For is this done by wreathing his body seven times round
   with elegant quickness.
For then he leaps up to catch the musk, which is the
   blessing of God upon his prayer.
For he rolls upon prank to work it in.
For having done duty and received blessing he begins to

consider himself.

For this he performs in ten degrees.

For first he looks upon his forepaws to see if they are
clean.

For secondly he kicks up behind to clear away there.

For thirdly he works it upon stretch with the forepaws
extended.

For fourthly he sharpens his paws by wood.

For fifthly he washes himself.

For sixthly he rolls upon wash.

For seventhly he fleas himself, that he may not be
interrupted upon the beat.

For eighthly he rubs himself against a post.

For ninthly he looks up for his instructions.

For tenthly he goes in quest of food.

Mother likes to show off her children; if I open the door,
something will come home. Behind my closed eyes, I picture
Emily's baby, Toby, whom I saw at six months and again at
thirteen months.

For I Will Consider My Grandson Toby
After Christopher Smart

For he has the sociability of his mother and the physical
strength of his father.

For dark skinned and haired, at first glance you would not
see how he resembles

his blue-eyed Uncle Seth, but for his big feet and big
hands.

For his uncle had big feet and big hands,

For this is so and I remember my son's spirit.

And this is also so: my son's fiancée, who restructures her
    life now without him,

came to visit Toby after six months away.

Firstly, Toby crawled to her circled arms and sat inside
    them as if they were a boat.

Secondly, Toby turned to look in her eyes and put his
    mouth over the end of her nose.

Thirdly, Toby did this again and fourthly again and
    fifthly once more.

Sixthly, we watched him take her inside of himself
    gobbling all that he could,

the playful desire for her that I saw in my son come again
    to earth.

And, seventhly, oh holy number, with tears in my eyes,

I have come to the page to consider Toby,

My daughter's now thirteen-month-old son, spirit of good
    news

And eighthly, how he is walking;

And ninthly how nothing makes him smile more than
    rising to his feet.

That is as far as I get.

The night after my flight home to Los Angeles, I dream
that my family has taken a ferry ride, and Kurt and I leave a
young Seth, maybe nine, in the charge of a friend who is also
on the ferry. When we dock and get off the boat, the friend
appears without Seth. Nobody knows what has happened to
Seth. Our hearts sink as we wait hours for news of him.

I write down this dream. I also write the names of Colorado
wildflowers I saw in Steamboat: columbine, lupine, and Turkish

blue. I note how, at this time of year, Colorado wildflowers will also be sprouting in my Port Townsend garden from a packet of seeds Seth once sent from school. Mother likes to show off her children. Feeling calm, I add to my poem:

> For tenthly, when he was six months old, I rode beside
> him, holding his hand from where he was strapped
> into his car seat and stared in his eyes that glazed safe
> and fighting sleep.

I go online to research the names of the flowers I listed in my notebook. Columbine, Aquilegia vulgaris, aquilegus a Latin adjective meaning "drawing water," spurs where the flower nectar collects. Lupine, Lupinus perennis, from the Latin lupus ("wolf"), once thought to deplete or "wolf" the mineral content of soil, actually enhances soil fertility by fixing atmospheric nitrogen into a useful form. Turkish blue, Veronica liwanensis, groundcover that may appear fragile, but is tough, grows well in full sun among other plants and between paving stones and on rock walls, equally at home along the Front Range and at 10,000 feet.

As I write about Toby, how can I not begin considering my baby, Seth? How can I not look at the pain of losing him? But how can I not look to the future? "Eleventhly," I whisper to myself, "Toby is the first of a new generation descended from me." May he always find water to quench his thirst, dew on green leaves to make him smile. May he find what he needs in the air and in the stars. May he grow in full sun, amidst family and many fine friends, as a small boy starting out, as a man taller than his mother.

CHAPTER ELEVEN

AT SUNRISE

And Now, 1987

This October, these leaves,
full moon over mountain
ridge of cloud.

In spring, 2003, Emily and Vijay learn that they will be moving from Northern California to Seattle. Kristen tells us she is considering moving to Seattle after her thesis and work in Rio are complete.

Kurt and I decide to leave Los Angeles and move to our Port Townsend house full-time. By inhabiting my retreat as our primary home, we are where Seth is alive for us in the quiet lapping of Discovery Bay, in the seeds of our garden, in the structure of the house he designed, in our memories of him growing up in the Northwest.

During college in Colorado, he sent many things he had made to Port Townsend. With the package of handmade cups and saucers, there had been a photo of him at a potter's wheel, and a note in his neat architect's block printing: "Also, a picture of my artist side."

Another note was sent one summer during junior high school when he was at bicycle camp on Orcas Island.

> Hey Dudes,
>
> I hope you're having as much fun as me. We are at Lakedale campground on San Juan. My writing is so bad because I'm dodging bees. The riding's been pretty good (of course I have the heaviest load).
>
> Love, Seth

I found these notes in the first days after Seth's death among my memorabilia stored in Port Townsend. I framed them and hung them behind my desk in my Los Angeles study. I knew they would be the last items I packed and the first I unpacked in Port Townsend. I imagined Seth sending one more card. It would say, *Mom, nothing happened to me that isn't going to happen to everyone else. I'm doing okay.*

Each December since 2000, we have returned to Port Townsend for the anniversary of Seth's death and bundled up to sit at sunrise on the benches dedicated to his love with Kristen. The doctors told us he was most likely dead upon impact that December 27, 2000, though his death certificate is dated December 28. Despite having no doubt that Seth had left us on December 27, Kurt and I wanted to get our ritual right.

The first year, we sat on those benches for two cold early mornings in a row. On December 27, 2001, the clouds parted when the sun rose making a brilliant red and pink display in the new sky. It seemed as if Seth sent that brilliance to remind us of our day at Gold Lake. Then, on December 28, the clouds remained a solid blanket, hardly acknowledging the sun's strength. Kurt and I decided we would recognize the 27th, along with Seth's birthday, as anchors in our year.

In 2002, Kurt and Emily and I sat on the benches on the 27th of December. As we approached the portico, built out over the benches in front of the Science Center's entrance, a hawk hovered as low to the roof as was possible without landing. He waited there while we walked to the benches and took off only when we reached the structure.

After that morning on the bench, Kurt and I flew back to Los Angeles to prepare to move. The days there had held gifts, too. Walking down the streets filled with people of all races and ethnicities, I saw the body build and distinctive walk, smile, and spirit of my son in African American kids and in kids from the French Academy in my neighborhood. On Seth's 28th birthday, I drove past a billboard that had just gone up with a large photo of a man concentrating. The expression between his eyes was Seth's.

I remember the shaman I saw in Port Townsend saying my boy was with Pythagoras, and then the way I read about his belief that all existing objects are fundamentally composed of form and not of material substance, that what gives the Unlimited form is the Limited. Whenever I see something of Seth in the people and images around me, I thank the Limited for giving Seth form again for a moment and for giving me ways to see my bodiless boy.

I like to imagine myself introducing Toby to the waters Seth loved, to the beaches where he collected limpets and sand crabs, watched people digging for clams and goeducks, to the trails he hiked to hot springs. I think of swinging in the oversized cloth hammock Seth loved to use on warm days with Kristen. I think of visiting the touch tanks at the Port Townsend Marine Science Center that Seth enjoyed writing his thesis about, and feeling the bumpy backs of starfish. Perhaps Toby will come in from my garden with a pocket full of snails, I think, as his uncle had when he was a toddler in Seattle.

Perhaps when he's a little older, Toby will go to summer camp at the Marine Science Center, which now maintains a Seth Bender Memorial Summer Camps Scholarship Fund. I hope Kristen will teach Toby how to kayak. I visualize the two of them out on Discovery Bay, in a double kayak and, later, side-by-side in two singles. I picture him with Kristen's future children and with a future sibling, all of them buoyant on blue water, all of them enriched by the spirit of a young man whose heart was large, whose heart still feeds them joy.

I picture myself waving from the beach near our house and sitting down on a driftwood log to write while I wait for them to return. Years ago and several houses before the house in Port Townsend, I explained to four-year-old Seth that I lived in a little house so I could spend my time writing. He called that house my poetry house. Now I am making my garden a poetry garden. There is already a post made of driftwood with a copy of my poem, "Sustenance," sealed between pieces of clear Lucite. I expect to stand beside it often, in the moonlight and in the daylight. I expect to build more posts and to seal more poems between more Lucite rectangles. Poetry is a way of healing for me because, through poetry, I learn what is true: when you search at the bottom, fish are stars, and when you search at the top, stars are fish, each clear despite the darkness. Look into Discovery Bay, I tell myself.

On December 27th, 2006

Kurt and I go, as we have for six years now, to watch the sun rise outside the Port Townsend Marine Science Center overlooking Admiralty Inlet to the Cascade Mountains. More often than not, we have witnessed exquisite sunrises. But even when there have been cloudy skies, subtle light brings divinity into relief, sometimes in the shape of animals in the large stones nearby. Other times, we've been accompanied, once again, by that hawk hovering over the portico that covers the benches.

This year, we take our places on the memorial benches a half hour before sunrise. We watch daylight break from behind a mostly cloudy sky, and at dawn we get up from the benches and walk across a small road to a long pier that extends into Admiralty Inlet. We hear a bird calling persistently, "Look my way! Look my way!" And when we do, we see a black bird sitting on top of a piling off to our right, a white patch on its neck, clear even from a distance. Then the bird flies south along the shoreline, a foot over the water, swallow-like, but at high speed. When it is out of view, I look north again and see our hawk circling.

At the end of the pier, we look out over Admiralty Inlet. The water below us swells and undulates in an unusual pattern and rhythm and with what seems, to me, a kind of affection. The swelling of the water becomes the backs of dolphins or of whales, so compelling I imagine riding one of them. I think of the orca totem Seth painted on the front of the kayak, the way it remains stored under our house, a spiritual foundation.

We watch a tugboat pulling a loaded barge from the Strait of Juan de Fuca into Admiralty Inlet. It looks like a friendly, furry monster from a children's book, with a crane that lies on its side for a tail and a bright lamp for an eye. For an instant, I think of standing here with the children Seth and Kristen would have had by now.

As Kurt and I walk back along the pier toward our car, I ask if he saw anything in the water, and he described being mesmerized by an unusual motion. He says the movement did not seem to correspond with any wave action or tidal currents. I feel certain that what we witnessed is there for us because of the change in our beings on this day, our heightened sense of belonging to a whole, the sense that allows us to locate Seth, to fully feel his presence.

At home, I get out my bird books with the hope of identifying the bird we had listened to and watched. I go to the Internet. Descriptions of the White Collared Vaux seem to match the bird we saw, though the species isn't said to winter here. As I look at the pictures of the black Vaux with a thick white patch at its neck, memories of Seth come—an eighth-grade boy standing outside of a French restaurant in his black pants and white shirt waiting for us to drive him home from his new busboy job and, from that same year, the sight of him standing on the school stage in black pants and white shirt to dance with his school's folkdance troupe, surprised to enjoy it so much.

I spend much of the rest of the morning re-reading poems I'd written about Seth over the years of his growing up. I resonate with the one I wrote in the months just after he left home for college, because it is about living without him, but feeling him everywhere, and it opens with a bird image:

Buying a Birthday Card for My Son
Just After He's Gone to College
For Seth on his 18th birthday

With each card I look at, I think of your phone calls,
        the way
they dart unexpectedly into my afternoons like
        sparrows.
I imagine the dorm room you describe, the rented
        refrigerator,
food carried from the dining hall, bed rigged to hang
        over your desk,
your stereo components integrated with ones your
        roommate brought.
As I listen, I think backwards, see you at 18 months
        in your cot
before tangerine striped wallpaper, your bib overalls
        on the floor,
pockets full of garden snails and twigs. Today, I hold
        a birthday
greeting book in my hand, flip the pages fast to see an
        animation

of candles lit and blown so hard the birthday cake
    slides into a lap.
Memories come of you sliding into my lap, pleading
    with me
to play cars, make engine noises, grind wheels over
    floors, watch
plastic smash into baseboards, of you running in
    cleats over muddy
Saturday soccer fields, chubby in your orange and
    black uniform.
Then I see you older, in summer carrying a
    windsurfing board
towards water, not telling us how afraid you are there
    might
be sharks and in the fall refusing rides I offer, insisting
    on using
your own two wheels, though it is dark and cold at
    midnight.
Then you get a perfect score on your driver's test,
    proud shoulders
straight as the bar on trapeze. You drive away and I
    pass through rooms
with your gifts from over the years, drawings in blue
    and red and yellow,
copper crab in the center of our dining table, deer
    shaped candleholder,
glass otters and hummingbirds, the book about
    mountain biking you
left for me to read since you aren't here to coax me up
    the high curbs.

At his benches, I told Seth, as I do every year, that I love him. Before Nootka roses and snowberry that form a backdrop to the Science Center building, below the fir and cedar tree-covered bluff that rises above it, I touched the love in me as strong as ever, and I thanked my son for the commitment and the energy he brought to this life.

As I write now, my thoughts turn to Kristen's coming marriage this September, just short of seven years since the accident, the amount of time a widow she had asked told her it would take to feel strong. I think of my four-and-a-half-year-old grandson, Toby, coming to visit us soon for "five days and four nights," as he excitedly describes his plans. I think of his brother, Raphael, now sixteen months old, able to speak many words, of which my favorite, of course, is "Ganma."

Seth would have loved designing and building for his nephews and his own kids; he would have loved visiting our home, where they could all hike and beachcomb and kayak. I know I would have loved watching him being a father. Honoring his spirit keeps my senses open to this world. It is essential if I am to make it up loss's high curbs and recognize the gifts in this life.

A couple of days after we sat on the benches, a visiting friend asks to read to us from William Blake's "Auguries of Innocence." These words stay with me:

> Man was made for Joy & Woe;
> And when this we rightly know
> Thro' the World we safely go.
> Joy & Woe are woven fine,
> A Clothing for the Soul divine;
> Under every grief & pine

Runs a joy with silken twine...
Every Tear from Every Eye
Becomes a Babe in Eternity...
The Bleat, the Bark, Bellow & Roar
Are Waves that Beat on Heaven's Shore.

Poetry gives voice to our bleats and our barks, our bellows and our roar; it is the voice that comes from inside the deepest experiences of our lives. It helps more than anything I know to weave what we most need, brilliant "clothing for the soul."

My sun is a sun boat on Discovery Bay. It comes to me each morning from the belly of darkness. My son cuts the hole through which light and poetry arrive. And I hold each poem I read and each poem I finish like a delicate vessel, since each contains something of always, exactly what I was searching for.

CHAPTER TWELVE

OF RUNOFF AND RUNNERS

July 2007

It is only weeks until we will leave to attend Kristen's wedding to Daniel. Daniel was a student at the University of Colorado, a year ahead of Seth and a biking buddy who spent time with Seth on trails on the weekends. When he graduated, he entered Columbia University Graduate School in Architecture, and he stayed in New York to work. One day, five years after Seth died, he decided to break off a long-term relationship that hadn't been working and return to California, where he grew up. He took a job in an architecture firm not far from the one Kristen began working for when she returned from her travels and finished her thesis.

Before long, he ran into Kristen at the birthday party of a mutual friend from school. He asked how Seth was. Kristen said that telling her story of loss at a casual meeting was painful. But she did tell Daniel. I try to imagine what she said, the breath she took to begin, or the way she didn't breathe as she spoke, the wavering quality again in her voice, or the whisper she might have spoken in. Daniel soon began courting her.

Today, I am re-reading parts of my book, *The Writer's Journal: Forty Contemporary Writers and Their Journals*, with a contribution from poet William Matthews. He starts his essay by stating that the notebooks of adored teacher and poet, Theodore Roethke, were not scrapbooks to "preserve something of the past, but a collection of scraps that yearn to be changed from the illusionary current form into something else, something future." Matthews writes that Theodore Roethke weeded his notebooks each year, "throwing out what no longer sparked. A few entries survived a dozen or more such cullings before Roethke put them to some use we can identify from his poems."

Roethke's sifting and saving aside, Matthews proposes that the real hope of a writer is that the scraps a writer comes upon and saves "might be changed, as fire converts matter to energy," or as in the work of "leaf mold on the forest floor." As I read the metaphors strung so closely together, I think about how the heat of fire is so different from the moist decaying of leaf mulch, about the searching Matthews was doing to find the right metaphor for what he'd experienced so often in his writing process.

I get up from my desk to check on my new berry patch, where the plantain, chamomile, trailing blackberry, and dandelions I turned with the soil in April are breaking through and flourishing again amidst the strawberries I planted. From four plants, forty more have sprouted, long runners everywhere, and from their many joints new leaves sprouting, stems taking root.

But each day I have been putting off weeding.

I stand with a hose, watering the patch. I think about water, not what sparks but what permeates the soil, carrying the fertilizer I've put on the plants' roots.

My mind wanders to other strawberry times. I remember visiting my daughter Emily in France when she was an exchange student, the abundance of strawberries served each night with cream at her three host families' dinner tables. As I watch the hose water fill gullies in the soil, my mind springs forward to the visit my husband and I made to Japan, when Emily was studying there. She warned us that, in Japan at a table with others, you are never to pour yourself a drink. You must instead be watchful for whose glasses are empty and fill them, yours being watched over by others. She said at first this is tiring, looking for how you are supposed to serve others, but then the custom makes life easier; without effort on your part, others are serving you.

Some of the hose water sprays into my new yellow plastic gardening shoes, but even with wet feet, I am on fire to write. What scrap will I work from while I wait for the pouring? What scrap will allow me to go deeper into the soil, without putting out the fire?

Despite the day's brightness, I am not wearing sunglasses. I squint into the light. Matthews says that white glare is the color of writing just before it hits the page. Perhaps the poem or essay is writing itself inside me.

The leaves of my strawberry plants deepen their green now that the white flowers and red berries are gone. Red. The bombs bursting in air. The glare in our hard-to-sing national anthem, its difficult range of an octave and a half. To write, one must be in touch with the ground and the glare, the range of what's between. One must let one's inner sight trickle down toward all that is vulnerable.

When Seth was a junior at the University of Colorado, his friends came to the kitchen in a converted fire station he shared with three others to work with hops and yeast and recipes downloaded from the Internet. Every Sunday evening, they sterilized jugs called carboys with iodine and siphoned week-old brew from one carboy to another to keep it from too much contact with sediments. They tasted and took readings of how the yeasts performed. They logged the sugar content and the ingredient amounts and re-jarred and labeled the yeast that had settled out. They bottled batches that had brewed for two weeks. They were pleased with all the apparatus they had gathered—strange corks for carboys topped with see-through tubular mazes, shiny copper tubing for handling the heated brew, and a gizmo they attached to their faucet to spray water deep into bottles and get them clean. They harvested pumpkin beer, oatmeal stout, and porters.

Once, Seth was on the front page of a local newspaper along with three other flannel-shirted Boulder boys, not for beer, but for architecture. The paper ran an article about the young men's mixed-use, medium density design for housing in a nearby prairie town, where development had so far only meant unfriendly four-lane highways for collecting what these architecture students called commuter runoff. The locals lobbied against the project for fear of too many people coming to live in the hamlet the students designed.

Their beer was delicious. After the city planning commission meeting, Seth couldn't decide whether to devote himself to beer or to architecture. He thought if he started a microbrewery somewhere with the attendant designer pub food restaurant and gave it five years, he could go back to graduate school in architecture, do three years of professional apprenticeship, and still be only thirty-one years old.

That's how old I was when Seth, aged six, said what I think of every day now: if he could, he would build me a house on wheels and drive me around so I could write and write. In all the years since he was born and the seven years since he died, I've been living in that house, albeit without physical wheels, but with the power to transport me, to help me slowly explore feelings and words and cruise new neighborhoods. Writing well is a slow, cumulative thing. A brewing.

This April, when I saw my five-year-old grandson's fingers in the dirt putting the strawberry plants we had just bought into the ground, I thought of Seth as the boy he was in the garden, his pockets full of snails and twigs. In May, my grandson was off to Legoland with his younger brother and parents, more his style, but the strawberries are something he remembers planting. Next spring, when the flowers are there, when the berries start and, once again, when they ripen, he'll visit with his little brother, notice the volunteer red poppies and the pink ones I do not weed away, like crepe paper over the strawberries and their runners, a party or a pageant.

But now, I break a yellowing leaf from the strawberry plant. I bury it in the earth, and I stay on my hands and knees to begin pulling plantain. When I see sorrel, a newcomer-weed to this patch, I reach for its long elastic roots.

William Matthews mused, "Some writers don't need journals because they have wastebaskets." My wastebasket is empty. My journal is on my computer. There, amidst the low-growing green, the tall volunteer poppies offer seeds for another patch of the ground I am wandering.

Over this past weekend, Kristen was visiting in Seattle, and she introduced us to Daniel.

"I can't get over this idea," she emailed soon after, "that it might just not happen for some reason and, even if it does, that marriage doesn't mean permanence."

I re-read the rest of the email, linger over Kristen's description of an antique oak English pub table and chairs we gave her years ago: "The table is due for a refinishing and needs a little work to get rid of a wobble."

I go back outside, continue weeding, making space for even more new shoots, knowing for both of us one garden will always grow in the center of another.

Just days before the wedding, Bob emails me that it would be nice if I had a poem for Kristen. Can I write one so fast, I wonder? Do I dare find out what is at the bottom of my heart just now when I am worried about the emotions we will feel when we get to the wedding?

I go back to the strawberry patch to weed. And then I know I have a poem to write for Kristen. I start with exactly what I am doing this morning:

Wedding Poem for Kristen Belt
September 8, 2007

Before I leave to see you marry, I check
the garden patch, where four strawberry
plants have over forty runners now,
new leaves and roots.
I kneel to pluck a yellow leaf, cover
it with fine soil, believing it will nourish
the others, deepen their greening.
Then I rise and linger in admiration
of such increasing lengths and feel the joy
you spread among us. From this lushness,
white flowers, sweet berries.

I show the poem to Kurt, and he prints it up on card stock, one copy for Kristen and one for her parents. We slip them into envelopes we will take with us.

December 27, 2007

Four months after the wedding, Kurt and I wake up early on this seventh anniversary of Seth's snowboarding accident. We fill our thermos mugs with coffee. As we approach the benches as usual on this day just before sunrise, a bird hidden in the trees behind the portico chirps; I am recognized, well greeted. I notice how much the four shore pines planted around the periphery of the portico have grown. I think about all the memories this spot has for me, including Toby exclaiming, "These benches are about my Uncle Seth and Aunt Kristen."

After the sun rises, we walk to our car. I look back at the benches and say thank you to the hawk, who has just swooped in over the portico, a little late this year, as if letting me know I am capable of finding Seth's spirit, all Spirit, myself, though he still does his job, flying low and circling.

EPILOGUE

Seth Michael Bender, October 1, 1975 – December 27, 2000

When various cults fought and overcame one another, the story of the god Seth changed as they sought to have their deities rise to the top. Although in some stories Seth is exiled to the desert, in later years, stories restore him as protector of the Sun Boat.

In translation, his name is considered to be either "one who dazzles" or "pillar of stability." These descriptors fit my child. He will never be banished from our hearts to the desert of forgetting.

On behalf of Seth, those who knew him and those who now know him through us, I want to preserve his legacy of supporting others. A portion of the proceeds from the sale of this book will be donated yearly to help expand the Seth Bender Memorial Summer Camps Scholarship Fund at the Port Townsend Marine Science Center. May many, many young people have a chance to treasure a connection to the outdoors, to all that lives there, and to the heart of a young man who could teach you to fly a kite, design a house, encourage others, and live with joy.

RESOURCES FOR THOSE WHO GRIEVE

During the first six months after Seth died, I spent much time reading books and articles about loss, as well as watching movies in which characters coped with the loss of children. My daughter, Emily, my cousin, Rabbi Rebecca Lillian, my friend, Cynthia Diament, and another cousin, Mindy Pollack sent books and titles I very much appreciated. Someone who knew me only through online instruction sent me a picture book inscribed for Seth that brought me much peace, and a friend of a friend, the children's book writer Ann Whitford Paul, sent one of her friend's children's books about the loss of a sibling. Kurt shared an Eva Cassidy song that deeply moved him. These gifts of art and information mattered very, very much. And they continued to come: songs over the radio, newsletters from the Tucson chapter of The Compassionate Friends, for which my friends Sam and Phyllis Turner were writing.

When you need to find a way, there are many who help. And I dug deep into what surrounded me. I watched Seth's tape of the film *Jacob's Ladder* again and again, because it is about a man who has died and because Seth had watched it over and over as a young adolescent. Of course, I studied poetry. Here is the list of work I most related to in the months and few years after Seth's death. I will always cherish the company of these human and inspiring works.

READINGS:

"Auguries of Innocence," by William Blake. This poem came to life as our friend, Pranesh Cadman, read it to us the end of December, 2006. As I was finishing this manuscript, these words became words to live by.

Duino Elegies by Rainier Maria Rilke, translated by Robert Hunter, Hulogosi Cooperative Publishers, 1989. I more than read Rilkes words; I worked with them, ingested them, changed as a result of them. In addition to Hunter's translation, I also read Stephen Mitchell's translation, Shambhala, Boston, 1992.

How to Read a Poem and Fall in Love with Poetry, by Edward Hirsh, Harcourt Brace and Company, New York, 1999. Working with Hirsh's words and the words of great poets, I began to reclaim my voice, to hear what it sounded like now that I was in grief.

In Lieu of Flowers: A Conversation for the Living, by Nancy Cobb, Pantheon Books, NY, 2000. My daughter gave me this book. In it, a young woman retraces her recently departed mother's young adult life by visiting the places where she had lived and worked. In her journey, she meets with many who, although they didn't know her mother, bring back portions of her mother's story and being. I gained faith that I would not forget my son.

Into the Valley and Out Again: The Story of a Father's Journey, by Richard Elder, 1996, Centering Corporation - Seasons of Grief Catalog of Grief Resources, 7230 Maple St. (72nd & Maple), Omaha, NE 68134, www.centering.org, Phone 420-553-1200. This father's narrative allowed me to enter the story of my grief.

Journey From Mount Rainier: A Mother's Chronicle of Grief and Hope by Judith Lingle, Ryan, Westview Book Publishing, Nashville, TN, 2006. Reading the story of someone who had traveled the route of this loss before me was important. I was with her every step of the way.

Making Loss Matter: Creating Meaning in Difficult Times, by David J. Wolpe, Riverhead Books, NY, 1999. This book helped me sustain my search for meaning in loss, my search for how I would continue in this life and be of service to my family and others.

More than Tears: Lifting the Burden of Grief by Janice Urie, Vantage Press, Inc., New York, 2005. The beginning of this book about the death of the author's school-age son in a bicycle accident was submitted as an essay to a *Writer's Digest Magazine* personal essay writing contest I judged a couple of years before Seth died. It was a winner. Janice went on over many years to finish her book, which provides solace to many. That I connected so strongly to the part she sent into the contest before Seth died stays with me.

"Saving the Indigenous Soul: An Interview with Martin Prechtel" by Derrick Jensen, *The Sun* magazine, April 2001. This is the interview that changed the direction of my grieving and allowed me to pursue the questions we need answered when unexpected loss arrives.

The Next Place, by Warren Hanson, Waldman House Press, Inc. Minneapolis, MN, 1997. A children's book with beautiful illustrations of the skies explains death as a part of the cycle of life.

This Might Help, by Phyllis and Sam Turner, The Turning Point, 7009 E. Paseo San Andres, Tucson, Arizona 85710, 2004, clearskys@cox.net. Several years after losing their 23-year-old son, this couple began writing columns for their local Compassionate Friends chapter that contained effective, gentle ways to deal with the grief that springs up daily. Later they collected them into this book that helps others bring life back into their days.

The Lovely Bones by Alice Sebold, Little Brown, New York, 2002. The novel concerns itself with grief and how it is and is not overcome by the protagonist's family. Written from the point of view of the daughter who has died, the book made me feel closer to the voice of my departed son.

Nadia the Willful by Sue Alexander, Knopf, New York, 1983. This children's story emphasizes the way speaking of the one who has died, in this case the protagonist Nadia's brother, is the way through grief because remembering is to have the company and love of the one who has died.

The Lessons of Love, by Melody Beatty, HarperCollins, New York, 1995 . Written from experiences after the death of her 15-year-old son, the book recounts the author's experiences of grief and provides twelve brief lessons about how to overcome despair and discover a passion for living.

FILMS:

In the Bedroom, directed by Todd Field, 2001, because the parents of a dead teen must move beyond hating the older woman who was dating him.

Jacob's Ladder, directed by Adrian Lyne, 1990, because as a young teen Seth watched it over and over and over again.

Life as a House, directed by Irwin Winkler, 2001, because a dying father does what he can to foster and nurture his son.

Moonlight Mile, directed by Brad Silberling, 2002, because the parents of a daughter who is killed take in the man they believe is her fiancé and feel very close to him.

The Son's Room, directed by Nanni Moretti, 2001, because a teenaged son dies and the family grieves.

What Dreams May Come, directed by Vincent Ward, 1998, because of the beauty in how we love though loss and parting are inevitable.

MUSIC:

"I Know You By Heart," sung by Eva Cassidy. Kurt found the song and when he plays it, we are moved to tears, perhaps because the recording artist too died young.

"September When It Comes," sung by Roseanne Cash. This recording captures the way we remember a loved one's soul.

AN ORGANIZATION:

The Compassionate Friends, Inc.; national information and ways to locate individual chapters at http://www. compassionatefriends.org/, P.O. Box 3696, Oak Brook, IL 60522-3696, Toll-free: 877-969-0010, PH: 630-990-0010, FAX: 630-990-0246.

ABOUT THE AUTHOR

Sheila Bender began writing poetry when her children were small. She continued writing and studying poems and, in 1982, graduated from the University of Washington with a Masters of Arts in Creative Writing. Since then she has taught at universities and community colleges in Seattle, Los Angeles, and Tucson, and has published nine books on writing and two books of poetry.

Today she lives with her husband in the Port Townsend house her son Seth Bender designed. She offers one-on-one help and classes through www.writingitreal.com. On the site, she also publishes *Writing It Real*, a weekly online magazine about writing from personal experience, launched in honor of Seth on October 1, 2002, the 27th anniversary of his birth.

Sheila supports the Port Townsend Marine Science Center's Seth Bender Memorial Summer Camps Scholarship Fund with donations from her book's proceeds and delights in knowing that many children and teens, her two grandsons among them, are attracted to the rich marine life on the salt water shores her son adored.

You can email her at info@writingitreal.com.

SETH BENDER SUMMER CAMPS SCHOLARSHIP FUND

Donated funds support scholarships for Port Townsend Marine Science Center day and residential camps for youth between 8 and 13 years of age. You can read descriptions of the programs at http://www.ptmsc.org/ by clicking on "camps." Donations to the fund may be made at the Center's website or by mail to the Seth Bender Fund, Port Townsend Marine Science Center, Fort Worden State Park, 532 Battery Way, Port Townsend WA 98368.

CPSIA information can be obtained at www.ICGtesting.com
Printed in the USA
BVOW082041120713

325500BV00001B/1/P